Dear T. Allan & Daphne,

May God Richly Bless You!

Elliot Tepp

You Can
Be Healed

Biblical Pathways to Healing

ELLIOT FOGGS

Many Will Be Healed Reading This Book.

WestBow
PRESS
A DIVISION OF THOMAS NELSON

WestBow Press books may be ordered through booksellers or by contacting:

WestBow Press
A Division of Thomas Nelson
1663 Liberty Drive
Bloomington, IN 47403
www.westbowpress.com
1-(866) 928-1240

Send healing stories to: eefoggs@live.com

ISBN: 978-1-4908-0434-7 (sc)
ISBN: 978-1-4908-0435-4 (e)

Library of Congress Control Number: 2013914230

Printed in the United States of America.

WestBow Press rev. date: 08/27/2013

CONTENTS

PART FOUR
YOU CAN BE HEALED THROUGH TECHNOLOGY

APPENDICIES

DEDICATION

THIS BOOK IS DEDICATED TO my wife, Kimberly, who for many years has gently, yet consistently encouraged me to write about my experiences. God has used her mightily in this.

And to the countless masses who suffer with illnesses of every kind, as well as the committed men and women in medicine who see to their care that they may know there is hope in Christ who is our healer.

God be merciful unto us, and bless us; and cause his face to shine upon us; Selah. That thy way may be known upon earth, thy saving health among all nations.

(Psalms 67:1-2, KJV)

Acknowledgements

I AM GRATEFUL TO MY wife Kimberly for her loving support and willingness to go through the hardships that come with this kind of ministry, and to my father and mother, Dr. and Mrs. Edward L. Foggs, for being a constant source of encouragement, strength and inspiration. They have seen up close and can witness to what the Lord has done. My siblings and other family members have offered timely words and sentiments that have helped me along the journey.

And I offer my heartfelt gratitude to the late Bishop Benjamin F. Reid, who was one of the first leaders in the Church of God to see something special in me and spoke prophetic words over my life that are coming to pass. His support, guidance and leadership have opened many doors, for which I will forever be indebted.

Special thanks go to Bishop Timothy J. Clarke for being the first Church of God pastor to welcome me into his congregation to bring the healing message. Thanks to Bishop G. A. Thompson, Apostle Rita J. Johnson, and the late Pastor Ken Tippen, true servants of God for believing in my ministry in the early stages and providing me with an open door. I am grateful for Dr. G. David Cox, who invited me to have healing meetings at Church at the

Crossing when I had been holding meetings in hotels, and my ministry was at a crossroads. Special thanks go to Pastor G. E. Studdard for encouraging me to move out in faith.

I am also thankful for the support of Pastor Robert A. Culp, Bishop C. Milton Grannum, and Dr. M. Tyrone Cushman who gave guidance along the way and exhibited great grace and generosity to me. I want to express sincere thanks and appreciation to the late Dr. E. Stanley Kardatzke. His vast knowledge of the medical industry, work ethic, and insight has been invaluable. The Lord put us together as close friends towards the end of his life for which I give thanks unto God.

I am indebted to the amazing staff at Thomas Nelson Publishing and Westbow Press for helping me to keep this project on track and meet the specified deadlines. Special thanks to Kenneth R. Wilson who was instrumental in the cover design, concept and layout.

In this book I offer many stories—some shared with me by friends, members of various church congregations, and people I've met along the way. I appreciate and acknowledge their contributions and support. Some of those mentioned in the book are people I have not met personally and, in a few cases, I've changed the names to protect the privacy of individuals. I give honor to whom honor is due. As the son of an international church leader and former pastor myself, I've listened to countless sermons and presentations, so in some cases I can't remember the exact source of a story. Thanks to all who have touched my life with their own. My intention in writing this book is to pass on these blessings with the prayer that God will be glorified.

FOREWARD

HEALING IS A TOPIC THAT is prominently addressed in Scripture—especially in the New Testament and in the life and ministry of Jesus. It also has received strong emphasis in many faith traditions. Interest in healing, however, has wavered from time to time between strong emphasis and de-emphasis. Fortunately, in the 21st century there is emerging a new and fresh interest in the subject in both religious and medical circles.

You Can Be Healed: Biblical Pathways to Healing is a volume that seeks to address various aspects of healing from Biblical perspectives. It is faith and prayer based and highlights Biblical methods of healing as practiced by Jesus and his followers in and beyond Biblical times. The author, Rev. Elliot Foggs, is my son and is an ordained minister of the gospel. He is gifted with a special healing ministry that, for several years, has found manifestation in many churches in and beyond the United States. In addition to the theological insights he shares, he includes personal experiences where God has used him to pray for many sick persons who have experienced healing. Some of these healings were gradual, while others were miraculous and instantaneous.

His approach is not anti-medical. He has interacted with medical personnel and shares experiences where medical doctors have acknowledged that some healings clearly were miraculous—beyond what their medical procedures were able to achieve. While it may be contended that all healing is divine, and it is, some healing is beyond the scope of medical science.

The author is not naïve. He recognizes and addresses the inevitably of death and speaks about that which is ultimate—*life* in Jesus Christ. I commend this volume as worthy of study and reflection, but most of all as a resource that can help readers receive their healing. He welcomes reports of healing as he shares the ongoing good news of the healing gospel and ministry of Jesus Christ.

Dr. Edward L. Foggs, General Secretary Emeritus,
Church of God (Anderson, IN)

INTRODUCTION

God heals and the doctor takes the fees.
—Benjamin Franklin

MANY PEOPLE ARE NOT AWARE that there are several methods available whereby healing can be obtained through faith in God and the Judeo/Christian scriptures. God's love and care for humankind is so great that he has provided various methods of healing. In this book, we will tell of one man's journey into healing ministry as well as examine common biblical healing methods. Each healing method we shall discuss was used by Jesus and his apostles, as well as other disciples.

In the scriptures, one can see that Jesus often used different methods when ministering healing to those in need. Sometimes he spoke to demons. Other times he laid hands on the person transmitting healing and miracle power to them. Still other times he would spit and make clay, anointing someone's eyes. A casual reading of the New Testament might lead one to believe that Jesus used strange and unorthodox methods in bringing relief to those suffering with sickness and disease, i.e., spitting and touching someone's tongue (Mark 7:33), or spitting on a person's eyes (Mark 8:23). But more careful study of the scriptures will reveal a uniform pattern in the methodology used by Jesus when ministering healing to the sick. We will identify methods of healing found in the New Testament, and encourage faith to reach out to God and receive the healing he so desires to give us.

It is not the purpose of this book to convey pristine theological arguments for the validity of spiritual healing although we are persuaded that the theological position we are taking is biblically sound. But rather this book is intended to accomplish two primary objectives. First, it should be understood upon reading "You Can Be Healed: Biblical Pathways to Healing", that sickness, as well as healing, are spiritual in nature and essence. They both flow from spiritual forces and spiritual principles. And, secondly, it is our prayer that this work will be an instrument in the hand of the Lord to spark spontaneous healing around the world. We intend to encourage and inspire those who read these pages to rise in faith and receive healing, knowing nothing is impossible with God.

The underlying premise for the position we are taking is that God's perfect will for all persons at all times is that they be healed. At first glance, this may seem like an unreasonable statement, especially in light of the fact that many people, including Christians, are ill throughout their entire lives. They receive prayer, visit multiple doctors, endure operations, and other medical procedures. They use herbs and vitamins, take prescription medications, use the latest gadgets and medical devices, and yet are never healed, but rather, die prematurely. And there are babies and small children who die of dread diseases that are cruel and distressing. But what must be made clear in all of this is that these things are not representative of God's perfect will. For we live in a fallen world under the influence of the prince of darkness. This sin-sick planet is reeling, due to the vast number of disease causing agents—environmental, physical, psychological and spiritual.

Over the past 30 years, a number of research studies have been published associating healing prayer with improved health outcomes. Yet, there is reticence within the medical community to discuss or deeply explore the spiritual side of healing. The primary reason for this reserved attitude is understandably a lack of knowledge by the medical profession on the subject. Another reason for the reluctance by religious physicians and scientists is a reverential fear, prohibiting secular medical science from intruding into the holy unknown. There seems to be a desire to preserve the mystery that is spiritual healing. To the religious friends who want to protect religiosity from the intrusion of the secular, to you we say God has nothing to fear from science. But science has much to learn from God present in science. Is it possible that God would even become a partner with science, physicians and scientists guiding scientific investigations leading to new discoveries on how best to heal the world?

Healing research can be hampered by antagonistic attitudes of some agnostic and atheist scientists and researchers who refuse religious faith as impracticable and feel there is nothing to claims of God's healing intervention in the lives of ordinary people. Of course, their position makes perfect sense when their baseline for a premise of existence and belief begins in the absence or non-existence of God. Some feel it is a waste of limited financial resources to invest in research projects that use unproven methodologies to investigate unexplored spiritual mechanisms which are neither easily defined nor clearly understood. Many feel that any claims of miracle or supernatural healing can be explained through psychology, the unexplainable explanation of spontaneous remission, placebo or some other accepted medical or scientific expression or construct.

There is, however, a profound and glaring question going unasked by those within the medical community. Today there are modern scientific research methods. The design and end of medical science is to bring relief to those suffering with disease and to "do no harm" as those entering the medical profession pledge through the Hippocratic Oath. Why wouldn't the institution of medicine desire to explore thoroughly the practices of the man credited with the most remarkable healing ministry ever recorded in the annals of the history of the world, Jesus Christ? For true atheists who consider the Bible a book of mythology or poetry, they cannot believe. However, the Bible is a God-breathed, inspired communiqué from the Most High to mankind. What about scientists that are believers? Fortunately some of them have stepped forward and conducted research on prayer's efficacy in a clinical setting. A time is coming, however, when spiritual methods will be thoroughly investigated, and all of humanity will be the beneficiary.

There must be reasons the medical industry has shied away from spiritual healing exploration. Of course, there is the obvious. They just don't know what they don't know. But beneath the surface is it possible that large pharmaceutical companies and the medical industry as a whole clearly understand that the moment they discover true healing at its root, that is, in the spirit, and attempt to spread it to humanity, corporate profits may be diminished due to less sickness and disease in the world? Fewer drugs to be sold? Could it be that very real answers lie in the spirit world?

Is it possible that the medical industry is trapped in a prison of its own design, having created mammoth organizations ever needing to secure product and revenue growth, new patents, new markets, novel medical procedures and devices? Although I highly honor the dedicated men and women who work in our healthcare system as administrators, doctors, nurses, technicians, etc., is it possible that in our modern world, there is such a focus on kowtowing to corporate boards and maintaining stock price and shareholder value that there is no time or incentive to seek the welfare of the most needy among us? Is it possible that due to market conditions and economic pressures things have gotten out of balance?

Is there any comparison or similarity between salvation of the soul and spirit and healing for the physical body, mind and emotions? Like salvation, healing is by grace through faith. And although the Bible is clear that it is God's will to save all those who believe on him, many cannot, will not, or for some reason or other do not receive God's gift of salvation. One would be hard pressed to support the idea through the scriptures that it is sometimes not God's will for souls to be saved upon demonstrating faith in Jesus Christ (2 Peter 3:9; Ezekiel 33:11). Is the fact that some never receive salvation an indication that God is unwilling to save? Can God's will to heal every person believing be established through the scriptures? These are some of the questions we shall explore.

All of humanity exists in a fallen condition due to the original sin of Adam, and yet the scriptures boldly declare that healing is for any, and all who will receive it by faith through the finished work of Christ. But before we go further let us look at some of the things that must be considered if one believes that at times, it is not God's will to heal.

First of all, if one is doubtful about God's will to heal, why should that person seek medical aid upon contracting a debilitating sickness? Shouldn't one rather simply bear with patience the malady. If it is not of a certainty God's will for one to be healed, then why should Christians in particular make attempts to be made well through medical science or other means? If it is not God's will to heal, then doctors, nurses and the entire medical industry are constantly potential instruments of evil. If it is not God's will to heal, the medical profession is working against the will of God to bring healing to those whom God, for his own divine purposes, does not wish to heal. For who is to say whether any given person is one of the lucky ones whom God chooses to heal? Rather one should remain in God's will by enduring the sickness until it runs its course.

Now, the above represents an absurdity far outside of reason as it is natural and sensible to make all efforts to relieve oneself of physical pain and suffering due to sickness if possible. But what typically happens in the Western world when illness strikes is one has all the medical tests performed, submits to the surgical procedures, takes the medications, changes habits, diet, exercise, etc. If no healing results from one's efforts after receiving all that medical science has to offer, it is presumed by most that God has spoken, and it must not be His will to provide the needed healing. To this we say there is a better way.

Secondly, if healing is not God's will for all, would there not be some reference in the New Testament where Jesus is asked to heal but clearly refuses and informs the inquirer that it is not God's will to heal them? The passage does not exist. Scripture affirms that Jesus came not to do his own will, but the will of his Father. Everyone Jesus healed—the blind, the lame, the maimed, the deaf and dumb, and demon possessed—was a reflection of the express will of his Father and not merely a proof of his divinity, as some theologians and scholars suggest. He never refused a single person who asked in faith, not one. And he taught his apostles and other disciples to do the same.

To say that it is not God's will to heal is to suggest a fundamental shift in God's treatment of mankind. Jesus healed all who came to him while he ministered on this earth (Matthew 8:16, 12:15). Even when confronted with healing requests from those outside of the Jewish faith—the Centurion (Matthew 8:5-13) and the Canaanite woman (Matthew 15:21-28)—Jesus didn't refuse ministering healing to them. When we look at the Bible, and recount its stories, sometimes it seems as if we forget that Jesus is still alive today and is healing multitudes as persons come to him in faith believing. The living Christ is the cornerstone of the Christian faith! One of the missing links in the world of healing and medical science today is a lack of acknowledgements of the fact of the resurrected and living Christ! The scripture records, "I am the Lord, I change not" (Mal. 3:6). If it is not God's will to heal supernaturally today, he has undergone a monumental change in character. He is no longer the God of Psalm 103:3, Psalm 107:20, Isaiah 53:4,5, Matthew 8:17, 1 Peter 2:24, James 5:14-15, or 3 John 2.

Finally, if one believes that it is not God's will to heal today, then one must admit that the opinion and conclusions drawn are based on one's own experience or the experiences of others and not on the scriptures, or church history but one's own subjectivity. Perhaps conclusions are based on information received from religious teachers over many years. Whatever the case, how can one reconcile a non-healing God, or a "selective healing" Christ with the scriptures? For Jesus Christ is the same yesterday, today and forever (Heb. 13:8). I am aware that this is a controversial and revolutionary position, but many of the teachings of Jesus are revolutionary.

Chapter One

SURPRISED BY THE SPIRIT

IN MARCH OF 2000 I had an appointment with the late Dr. Steven Williams, then head of oncology for Indiana University (IU) School of Medicine. My purpose for setting the meeting was to request and gain approval and assistance to conduct healing prayer research in the medical school. Upon walking into his spacious office, he motioned for me to sit down in a chair right in front of his large wooden desk, which appeared to be made of cherry wood. As he looked at me over his partial rimmed reading glasses, we shared introductions and pleasantries. Then I got to the purpose of my visit—the reason for which I had scheduled the meeting. I introduced him to the Christian healing ministry as I understood it and suggested that studying healing principles from a biblical perspective may provide benefits to the cancer patients under his care.

His response was less than glowing. So, I began asking questions, attempting to discover whether he was a man of faith. And although he was neither antagonistic nor unfriendly, he was quite reserved. And no wonder, he didn't know me or my true motivation for being in his office that day. As our meeting continued he seemed to be holding everything in, not letting me into his world. It felt to me as if he had on what has been termed a "poker face". And he wasn't about to let me see the cards in his hand. After attempting to probe, prod, and postulate to no avail, I concluded that our visit was proving unfruitful and that there was no need to keep going. This was the first time we had met, which may have accounted for his reserved demeanor. In my mind I began planning my escape. I pictured just how I would end the meeting to both save face and secure Dr. William's comfort level with the final outcome.

He was responding to one of my questions, and honestly I wasn't listening to his response. Mentally, I was working on my exit strategy, waiting for him to finish so I could wrap up the meeting and excuse myself. Suddenly the Spirit of the Lord spoke to me! Now for some I know this may be foreign. It may seem unlikely, preposterous, even sacrilegious. However, I know of no other way to explain what happened next. And after seeing the path my life has taken I have no doubt who it was that spoke to me that day in late March. In the middle of planning my exit, I was arrested by a voice that said, "Tell him to look out the window". I argued within myself, this makes no sense. Tell him to look out the window for what, I replied. I didn't want to do it. And again the voice said, "Tell him to look out the window".

Dr. Williams was still speaking, finishing his response to one of my earlier questions. He appeared pleased with his answer, through which he was assuring me of his vast knowledge of cancer treatment and care—a knowledge that far exceeded my own. When he finished speaking, against my better judgment I said, "Dr. Williams, look out the window".

I had no idea what I would say next. I watched as he turned slowly to his right to look out of the large picture window that brightened his office. I too looked out the window as if straining for further instruction. But as I did I noticed (in my hurry to get to the meeting that morning, I hadn't really paid much attention earlier) it was a bright, sunny, gorgeous day. The sky was a rich color of blue, and there was hardly a cloud in it.

The sun beamed spreading its warmth across campus. And a tree just outside Dr. Williams' window cast a shadow monitoring the amount of sunlight allowed in the room. If one looked just to the left of the trees, the sight was beautiful to behold. The sun was shining on the grass which was a fresh, spring bud green having rebounded from the harsh winter just past.

After I had asked Dr. Williams to look out the window, the words started to flow, and I began to say, "You see the trees, the sun, the sky and the grass? In the Christian faith, we believe all of these things were created by God." Then I asked him, "Are you following me?" He said, "Yes." I continued, "So everything you can see outside was created by a God who is invisible and cannot be seen." I asked again, "Are you following me?" He said, "Yes." I then said, "In the case of cancer, it can be seen under a microscope and in X-rays. I believe there is something invisible behind the cancer giving life to it. You see, cancer grows and only living things grow. If by spiritual means you could restrain or destroy the life force behind the cancer, then you could eradicate the cancer." I had never heard anything like this before and was surprised these words were coming out of my mouth. Although I was familiar with the concept in principle, the specific application for cancer was completely new to me.

Dr. Williams' reaction to this paradigm shift was amazing to me. To this point I had never heard anyone postulate that cancer cells, atoms and subatomic particles have a root and foundation that does not originate in the physical world. So, atoms and subatomic structures are built upon spiritual, not natural principles. If this truth could be submitted as theory and proven in a clinical setting, it could change the way people think about disease, medicine, medical research and medical science in general. Dr. Williams' posture changed. His shoulders dropped, and he began shaking his head slowly from side to side as tears welled up in the outer corners of his eyes and then rolled down his cheeks. I had no idea what brought about this reaction.

He then repeated, over and over, nine words that changed the meeting, and my future. "There's a lot of truth in what you're saying. There's a lot of truth in what you're saying. There's a lot of truth in what you're saying. There's a lot of truth in what you're saying." Finally, he admitted as if he were in a confessional with a priest, "I know we can do more for our patients." He then proceeded to give me names of the department heads in the IU School of Medicine and suggested that I speak with each of them. Subsequently, I met Dr. Vimal Patel and Dr. Palmer Mackie, who ran the school's Complementary and Alternative Medicine (CAM) program. Dr. Patel would eventually ask me to lecture in the program. Also, I was able to meet with Dr. Douglas Zipes, then head of cardiology, who told me a story where he was recruited to attend a healing meeting as a plant, but later left the meeting feeling more like a believer than a skeptic. I began working with his team to put a prayer healing study together.

I met Dr. Kenneth Brandt, then head of rheumatology. He and his assistant met with the late Dr. E. Stanley Kardatzke, Dr. Edward L. Foggs and me. We discussed using prayer and other biblical healing methodologies for arthritis patients. While in the meeting, Dr. Brandt received an important phone call, and had to leave the room momentarily. While he was gone, his assistant motioned to us drawing us closer. Then she told us her story. She told us how when she was a young girl her baby brother had tuberculosis and was dying.

One day she was watching TV and Oral Roberts was on conducting a televised healing service. She then disclosed to us that at the end of the service Rev. Roberts asked all that were sick to place their hands on the TV screen for healing. She said she carried her brother in her arms to the TV and placed his hands on the screen. She then reported to us that her brother did not die, but was completely healed! Then she said, "I'm so glad you are looking into doing research on healing and prayer." These events culminated in the development of a unique spiritual healing research proposal created by Dr. Kardatzke and me.

Chapter Two

YOU DO HAVE FAITH

FAITH IS A SUBJECT OFTEN discussed in both religious and non-religious circles, but what is it—really? Scripture teaches that faith is belief in, dependence on, confidence in God or religious teaching. It is also described as substance, or spiritual material or reality. Now we will not be addressing natural human faith, as the confidence one has that a chair will hold one's weight upon sitting down. All have that kind of faith.

Biblical faith can be described as spiritual material that manifests or appears in various forms and ways in the mental, physical, and spiritual world. Hebrews 11:1 says, "Now faith is the substance of things . . . ." In John 1:1-3 it is recorded that, "In the beginning was the word and the word was with God and the word was God. The same was in the beginning with God. All things were made by him and without him was not anything made that was made." In other words, all things in the material world were created by the Word of God, or the Word of God was the spiritual substance of the things that were made in the beginning. Now we know that according to the scripture the Word of God is spirit first. In other words, everything that was created in the beginning was created by the invisible spirit God through the use of words, or better yet, "The Word".

Let me again suggest at this point the following paradigm shift which arose from reflections on my meeting with Dr. Williams. Cells, atoms and subatomic particles, which make up the building blocks of all other things, find their foundation not in the physical world, but in the spiritual world. For through scripture and by faith, we understand that the world, and everything in it, was created by God. So, the original material creation of earth was made by a spirit, and that spirit is the origin of all things. Even the smallest particles of matter must of necessity have a spiritual foundation beneath the subatomic.

Because of the scriptures referenced above found in John chapter one and Hebrews chapter 11, it seems plausible to suggest that in some cases faith and the Word of God can be synonymous terms. If one were to interchange the phrase Word of God with faith in the Hebrews passage, it would then read, "Now the Word of God is the substance of things hoped for, the evidence of things not seen." This rendering would be true to other passages of scripture. What conclusions can be drawn from making this kind of interchange?

Is it possible that when someone is seeking healing through faith—faith in God—he must actually exercise faith in the Word of God. God and his word are one, i.e. ". . . the word was with God, and the word was God . . ."

(John 1:1) So, God's word can do anything God can do including bringing healing to the sick. This would explain in part why Satan has for centuries been attempting to invalidate the Word of God, which would invalidate God himself! God and His word are inseparable.

When someone truly believes, the Word of God then becomes the substance, or spiritual material, from which the person's healing will be manifested. Words are spirit. The practice of exercising one's faith begins by meditating on the Word of God. When one has faith in God's word, it is the same as having faith in God himself. Correct meditation produces a belief in the heart, which when spoken out of the mouth and acted upon releases the power of faith producing healing for the believer.

When one is seeking healing through faith then, the Word of God becomes the spiritual substance or assurance that he or she can and will receive the healing that is hoped for but has not yet been manifested. The only evidence needed is a promise of healing in the Word of God. God's word, in turn links a person to the spiritual power that eliminates impossibilities. We put our trust and confidence in God's word. And as we have said, that is the same as trusting in God. There is no difference. It is, therefore, imperative to discover what the Word of God has to say about healing from disease so that one can have something to put one's faith in, or something upon which to exercise one's faith.

It is impossible to exercise true scriptural faith outside of the known will of God. God's will is revealed in His word. And God never requires us to have faith for something which he has not already promised. True faith for healing is based on promises found in scripture. And, when in proper operation, faith will cause one to act like the Word of God is true, accurate, trustworthy, and reliable. An elementary definition of faith is simply acting like the Word of God is true. Faith is a law that works every time it is applied correctly.

A key scriptural reference, found in Romans 10:17, tells us that faith comes by hearing the word of, or about God. When the human spirit is exposed to the Word of God, faith is produced. Exposure to the Word of God builds a capacity for faith. Acting on the Word of God strengthens one's faith. In other words, meditation gives greater capacity for acting on the Word of God. It is the acting we are after, but only when one has a firm belief in the heart.

For example, reading books on exercise, nutrition, and fitness will not give one a strong, healthy body, but eating right, going to the gym and working out will. However, reading books on the subject will increase the likelihood that a person will eventually get to the gym, and change their diet. In the same way, meditation builds an inner image of oneself in the light of scripture rather than natural surroundings. A person may begin to see himself healed when as yet all the symptoms of sickness remain. One can see the reflection of a healed person through the mirror of the Word of God. This inner image created by meditating on the Word engages or activates the faith substance on behalf of the sick person. This is not to suggest that one should deny the existence of their disease. That would be foolish and potentially harmful, possibly fatal. Rather, one should acknowledge the truthfulness of God's word in spite of their physical condition, allowing truth to conquer facts.

There are factual conditions and symptoms associated with all disease. However, there is a higher reality called truth that actually has the power to change facts surrounding any physical condition. When one engages the truth through meditation, actions that lead to healing follow. John 17:17, along with other passages, tells us that God's word is truth, or ultimate reality. Faith is a spiritual force, or spiritual substance obtained by hearing the Word of God. It is released by one's words and actions. The basic faith principle consists of acting on, and saying with the mouth what one firmly believes in the heart, or spirit. It is a spiritual law, which can be enhanced in an individual's life through continued practice.

Chapter Three

GOD'S WILL FOR YOU

A S A YOUNG MAN IN college, I learned a valuable lesson about the common cold, flu, and other illnesses. Like most people, I have had my share of these ailments. In 1980, I was just beginning to study faith and healing. Sometimes I would go to the Wabash River in Terre Haute, Indiana, home of Indiana State University and sit on the river bank for hours reading the scriptures. This was where my education and fascination with healing began. Cold and flu symptoms are easy to detect. That feeling one gets just before a cold or flu grips the body is universal, the scratchy throat, agitated sinuses, watery eyes. One can feel a cold coming on long before the complete symptoms are apparent.

It was during this time I discovered it was not God's will for me to catch a cold. Now, I know how that sounds. And I am aware that not everyone can accept this. Let those who can accept it accept it. One day at school while I was crossing the street headed from my dormitory to the campus gymnasium I felt cold symptoms coming on me.

My throat, head, and sinuses began exhibiting all of the classic signs of an upcoming bout with sickness. My first thought was, oh boy I'm catching a cold. I began to think of all the things that go with colds—the medicine, the icky feeling, runny nose, sore throat, clogged sinuses and just the complete misery of it all.

I was getting ready to say: I'm catching a cold. When from somewhere deep inside me these words came to mind, I don't receive this. At the time, I don't know why I said it, but I said those words out loud. I said, "I don't receive these symptoms." When I did, within a few moments, almost instantly, every symptom vanished. Days and weeks went by, and the symptoms never returned. Over the years, I have practiced this, and though I haven't been perfect at it, I haven't had full blown cold symptoms in many years. Thank the Lord for his grace. We can all learn to resist sickness as we understand God's will as revealed in his word.

Knowing God's will in regards to healing is of extreme importance since faith for healing cannot be exercised where the will of God is not known. For a person pursuing the will of God for one's life, if that person is unsure of exactly what God's will is, there will always be doubts and uncertainty about that thing for which they are trusting the Lord—healing in this case. Doubt if allowed to go unchecked can cripple faith.

The scripture in the book of James says that when asking of God, we must ask in faith, nothing wavering (James 1:5-6). Here, he is talking about asking for wisdom. But, the principle he mentions in chapter one also applies to healing.

So, we know that it is God's will to give us wisdom because the scripture says He will give it to us if we but ask Him. Likewise, we know that it is God's will to heal us because His word tells us that we can call for the elders of the church, have them anoint us with oil and pray the prayer of faith over us. And "the prayer of faith shall save (heal) the sick and the Lord shall raise him up . . ." (James 5:14, 15).

James also instructs us to pray for one another that we may be healed. To exercise Bible faith for healing successfully and consistently, we must be thoroughly convinced it is God's will that we be healed. If one doubts, he becomes like "a wave of the sea driven with the wind and tossed" (James 1:6). And as such, one should expect to receive nothing from the Lord in the area of healing, being double minded. Being persuaded of God's will to heal is one of the secrets to receiving healing through faith.

Chapter Four

YOU CAN ACCESS HIS NAME

BUILDING UPON THE PREMISE THAT it is God's will to heal, let us now move on to various methods of receiving healing identified in scripture. The first method we shall mention is the name of Jesus. The supporting scripture is found in John 14:12-14. In preceding verses Jesus shares with his disciples that the works he is performing are actually being accomplished through him by his Father. The verses do not identify to which works Jesus is referring, but in earlier chapters we see Jesus walking on the sea, healing a man born blind, and raising Lazarus from the dead. Verses 12 through 14 read:

"Verily, verily I say unto you, he that believeth on me, the works that I do shall he do also, and greater works shall he do; because I go unto my Father. And whatsoever ye shall ask in my name, that will I do that the Father may be glorified in the son. If ye shall ask anything in my name, I will do it."

At a glance, it could appear that these verses are talking about prayer. But they are not. In the above scriptures, Jesus is talking about the ability of those who believe in His name to do the same works He accomplished. Ephesians 1:20-23; Philippians 2:9-11; and Matthew28:18 all convey the fact that God the Father has attributed all authority in heaven and the earth to the name of Jesus. The name of Jesus subdues arthritis, AIDS, blindness, deafness, heart failure, kidney disease, cancer, and any other disease known or unknown. Diseases have been given names by men. And, whatever the name of the disease state, it is inferior and subject to the name of Jesus, given to us by God. Thus, healing is readily available through that name. In the third chapter of the book of Acts, we see this healing principle in action. The chapter opens with Peter and John going into the temple to pray. Then in verse 2 we read:

"And a certain man lame from his mother's womb was carried, whom they laid daily at the gate of the temple which is called Beautiful, to ask alms of them that entered into the temple. Who seeing Peter and John about to go into the temple asked an alms. And Peter, fastening his eyes upon him with John, said, look on us. And he gave heed unto them, expecting to receive something from them. Then Peter said, 'Silver and gold have I none, but such as I have give I thee: In the name of Jesus Christ of Nazareth rise up and walk.' And he took him by the right hand, and lifted him up: and immediately his feet and ankle bones received strength. And he leaping up stood, and walked, and entered with them into the temple, walking, and leaping and praising God."

This miracle resulted in stirring up a good deal of excitement, and everyone wondered what happened and how this wonderful deed was done. The apostles explain that it was not because of their own holiness or any special power they possessed that the man was healed. Some today think that the apostles had that kind of power and no one else can do what they did. But verse 16 spells out exactly how the man was made whole. "And his name through faith in his name hath made this man strong, whom ye see and know: yea the faith which is by him hath given him this perfect soundness in the presence of you all."

So, one can see that faith in the name of Jesus is what caused the lame man to be healed. And faith in the name of Jesus will cause people to be healed today. The weakest, most feeble believer around has the same authority over sickness the apostles had and can resist sickness and disease in the name of Jesus. There is power in the name of Jesus! Hardly a day goes by in my personal life where the name of Jesus isn't used to resist temptation, oppose a threatening physical symptom, control the thoughts of my mind, or recover from a satanic attack. What would those in Christ do without that great name?

Chapter Five

DON'T EVER STOP PRAYING

PRAYER IS THE MOST RECOGNIZED method of receiving healing amongst all religions today. Oddly enough, even those who do not believe in healing prayer pray at times for God to heal the sick. Often they do it out of obligation. Maybe someone is pastoring a congregation where it is expected that one should pray for the sick—so one does. But that person doesn't expect any results from healing prayers, and when he gets none, he surmises that prayers rendered for the sick do not work. In the rare cases where people may get healed, it is attributed to a sovereign act of God alone. All healing is by grace. There is a healing agent in mankind naturally placed in us from creation. It is a gift from God. However, what we are discussing goes beyond human nature. It is supernatural and yet is still a gift unearned and freely given from God, an extension of His boundless grace. He hears and answers our prayers for healing because of His love for us.

Some time ago I had a telephone conversation with a medical doctor and Harvard graduate. He is a brilliant academician and medical professor at a prestigious U.S. university. He attempted to convince me that God was too busy to listen and respond to individual prayers for healing. He had written a paper on the subject that was published in a popular medical journal. His premise was that God was too big for that and had more important things to do like keeping the stars and planets aligned, etc. When people compare God to humans in terms of ability they often make this mistake, especially intellectuals and the exceptionally gifted ones among us. Because our schedules are packed and we often have difficulty getting everything accomplished that needs to be done, we sometimes unwittingly impose those limitations on God. But God is unlimited, infinite. His knowledge is unsearchable and His ways past finding out. He has made available to us a healing grace that can be received through prayer.

The early church prayed to God for healing. Healing, signs and wonders added to the boldness of their witness for Christ, according to Acts 4:29–30. It reads, "And now, Lord, behold their threatening: and grant unto thy servants, that with boldness they may speak thy word. By stretching forth thine hand to heal; and that signs and wonders may be done by the name of thy holy child Jesus."

An earthquake even occurred following the prayer for healing and boldness. Oh that our prayers for healing would shake the earth. So, one can see it is scriptural to pray for healing. In John 16:23–24 Jesus gives his followers specific instructions on prayer: "And in that day ye shall ask me nothing. Verily, verily I say unto you, whatsoever ye shall ask the father in my name, he will give it you. Hitherto have ye asked nothing in my name: ask and ye shall receive, that your joy may be full."

Through simply asking the Father in the name of Jesus, we can receive healing. This is a promise from Jesus. Mark 11:22–24 also addresses this issue of believing prayer. Finally James 5:15 mentions prayer in specific relation to healing. Prayer for healing is scriptural, and believers have a right to expect God to heal them when the prayer of faith is offered on their behalf. And concerning God's will regarding healing, the Holy Spirit says through James, "Confess your faults one to another and pray for one another that ye may be healed . . ." (James 5:16). With this direct admonition, wisdom asks the question, would God tell us to do something that is not His will?

If at times it is not God's will to heal us, and yet he tells us to pray for healing, then he is working against himself. He is purposely getting us out of His will by telling us through His holy written word to pray for something that he has no desire or plan to give us. That is not an act of love and mercy, but rather cruel and heartless. If it is not God's will to heal some people, why in James does He tell believers to pray for one another to be healed? Was it just for some therapeutic exercise? It is reasonable to conclude that He told us to pray for healing because God wants us to be healed. God wants you to be healed! Our need is to learn how to cooperate with him in prayer to receive our healing. Prayer will produce healing. But fervent, effective prayer is work—real work, and its rewards can be enormous. Sometimes it is easier to say, forget it. It must not be God's will to heal me. We must not be apathetic, but through discipline, dedication and diligence press onward into prayer.

Chapter Six

JESUS TOOK YOUR PLACE

FOR THOSE WHO CAN ACCEPT it, God actually took care of our sicknesses and diseases through the blood sacrifice and resurrection of Jesus Christ. In the great prophetic chapter, Isaiah 53:1 begins by asking a profound and far reaching question, "Who hath believed our report?" What report? The report says, "Surely he hath borne our griefs and carried our sorrows: yet we did esteem him stricken, smitten of God and afflicted. But he was wounded for our transgressions, he was bruised for our iniquities: the chastisement of our peace was upon him and with his stripes we are healed." (Isaiah 53:4–5) Jesus was our substitute. He gladly took the punishment we deserved, and not without purpose. In verse 10, it reads, "Yet it pleased the Lord to bruise him: he hath put him to grief . . ." or, he hath made him sick!! His soul became an offering to God for the sins of the whole world.

One must understand that Jesus was made sin that we might be made righteousness (2 Cor. 5:21). He was made sick that we might be made well and whole spiritually, mentally, emotionally, and physically. It may be true that many will not experience this perfect blessedness, wholeness and peace until they pass over the great spiritual divide into eternity. However, it is also true that healing and wholeness are available now in this present world for any and all who will receive them by faith.

In Matthew 8:16-18 we read, "When the evening was come, they brought unto him many that were possessed with devils: and he cast out the spirits with his word, and healed all that were sick: that it might be fulfilled which was spoken by Isaiah the prophet, saying, himself took our infirmities and bare our sicknesses." This scripture reveals that Matthew understood Isaiah 53 to mean that Jesus literally carried our sicknesses away. It is interesting that in many scripture passages the Lord gives just enough information for one to believe. One must always choose what one will believe. The truth is Jesus bore our sicknesses so we would not have to bear them. He bore our sin so that we could be made righteous. Now we can resist sin and triumph over it. He bore our sicknesses so that we could be made well. Now we can resist sickness and disease and triumph over it. God is, and has always been, concerned with the whole man, not just the saving of the soul. For the God who created the soul and spirit created the body also.

For those who can accept it, in God's mind we are already healed and simply need to receive what he did at Calvary as efficacious for us. Many think they are waiting for God to heal them. When in fact, God is waiting for them to believe the words He has spoken. In

1 Peter 2:24 it reads, "Who his own self bare our sins in his own body on the tree, that we, being dead to sins, should live unto righteousness by whose stripes ye were healed. Peter refers back to Isaiah 53 and writes as if our healing is an event that has happened in past time. So the cross and subsequent resurrection was the culmination of complete salvation for the whole world. Now it is up to men, women, boys and girls everywhere to accept what has been provided for them through the sacrificial death of Jesus, i.e., salvation and healing for the whole man.

There is a story that illustrates this point well. A pastor was holding a healing meeting in a certain city. Just after one of the services was over, a woman came up to him in a wheelchair requesting prayer for healing. She had been diagnosed with rheumatoid arthritis and had been confined to her wheelchair for seven years. The pastor had been ministering under a healing anointing during the service, but the anointing to minister had lifted. So, he asked the woman to come back to the next service, and he would minister to her then. But she told him that she had to leave the city and could not attend any other services. So he sat down with her in front of the pulpit and began to speak with her.

He started off by saying, "My sister, did you know you're healed?" He said she looked at him in disbelief as if to say; Man, are you crazy? Can't you see me sitting in this wheelchair? But after a moment she said, "Oh, am I?" He said, "Yes, you're healed and I'll just prove it to you by the Bible." He took her to 1 Peter 2:24 and had her read the verse out loud. She read, "Who his own self bare our sins in his own body on the tree that we being dead to sins should live unto righteousness: by whose stripes ye were healed." He asked her to read it four different times. After she read it the last time he said, "Sister, I have a question for you. Is the word 'were' past tense, present tense, or future tense?" She said, "Past tense." He said a look of surprise came on her face, and it seemed as if her face lit up (remember Psalm 119:130 says, "The entrance of thy word giveth light"). Then she said, "Well if I was healed, I am!" The pastor said, "That's what I want you to believe."

Then the pastor said to her, "Sister will you do what I tell you to do?" She said, "I will if it's easy." Of course, everyone is looking for something easy. He said, "This is the easiest thing you've ever done. I want you to lift both hands and begin to praise God because you are healed—not going to be, but are!" Most people with natural human thinking would have reasoned and said, yeah, but I'm not healed. But he said he wishes we could have seen that little old lady. She immediately lifted both hands and began to say, "I'm so glad I'm healed. Lord, you know how tired I got sitting around in this old chair, but now I'm so glad my limbs are healed. I'm so glad my knees are healed. I'm so glad I don't have to be waited on any more!" Next the pastor spoke to the congregation and said, "Let's all praise God with her." And as the church was praising, he turned to the woman and said, "Now my sister rise and walk in Jesus' name." And in front of more than 800 witnesses the woman jumped out of the chair and ran around the whole church. Praise the Lord, by His stripes we are healed!

Chapter Seven

WHY LAY HANDS ON THE SICK?

LAYING ON OF HANDS IS evidently the main way Jesus ministered healing during his earthly ministry. There are several scriptures one could use to demonstrate this point, i.e., Mt. 8:3, 15; Mk. 5:23, 6:5, 7:32, 8:23-25; Lk. 5:13, etc. Hebrews 6:2 tells us that the laying on of hands is a principle doctrine of Christ. The phrase, principle doctrine, carries with it the meaning that the laying on of hands is chief in the order of God's divine expression. In other words, laying on of hands is a primary way God uses to express Himself to mankind— one of the dominant means He uses to manifest or reveal Himself to us.

The ministry of laying on of hands was taught by Jesus, and he commanded us to continue practicing this ministry in the church. All believers should be actively involved in laying hands on the sick today! In Mark 16:15-18 one can read, "He that believeth and is baptized shall be saved, but he that believeth not shall be damned. And these signs shall follow them that believe, in my name they shall cast out devils, they shall speak with new tongues; they shall take up serpents; and if they drink any deadly thing, it shall not hurt them; they shall lay hands on the sick and they shall recover."

All believers have the right to lay hands on the sick and expect them to recover. Now notice Jesus said, recover, which in most cases indicates a process. Not everyone is instantly healed. Some people think that in Jesus' ministry everyone was healed instantly. But they were not. In Luke 17:11-19 the Bible records that the ten lepers were healed as they went and in John 4:46-54 one finds that the nobleman's son began to amend from the moment Jesus spoke. But he went through a healing process of getting progressively better. It wasn't instant.

Towards the end of a healing meeting in Michigan, a man came forward for healing prayer and to have hands laid on him. He was deaf in one ear and asked if I would pray for him. After raising my hands, I stuck my finger in his ear and commanded the deaf spirit to come out as I had done in healing services many times before. Nothing happened. He left the meeting just as deaf as he was before he came up for prayer. It can be discouraging when one sees people coming forward for prayer; hopeful to get help and then apparently receive none. It is disheartening.

But experience has taught me never to count God out. No matter how hopeless things appear, nothing is too hard for the Lord! In this particular case, the man returned to the service the next day to announce that he was a bit down because his ear wasn't instantly healed. But when he went back to his room, in the middle of the night, suddenly his ear popped open, and he could hear clearly. When he came back to the meeting on the following day he testified that he could hear everything normally.

Some people become confused in their thinking on this issue. They feel if their healing doesn't happen instantly it really is not God doing the healing. Or they think faith and prayer are not working, but nothing could be further from the truth. Keep believing and you will see the healing. Understand that for various reasons there is often a process in our healing, and that process is just as big a part of our healing as the actual relief from pain, suffering, sickness and disease. There are three primary scriptural purposes for the laying on of hands. They are:

1. Provides a point of contact for one to release one's faith (Mark 5:25-29).
2. Provides a channel through which the gifts of the Spirit can operate (Acts 19:11).
3. Provides a way for spiritual gifts to be imparted (2 Timothy 1:6).

Because the Spirit of God dwells inside of every believer, anyone who has a living faith in Jesus Christ can lay hands on the sick, and they will recover. Through the law of contact and transmission, the Holy Spirit that dwells inside will flow from one's hands into the sick person and drive out their sickness and disease. In other words, when a believer lays his hands on the sick the Spirit that the person is anointed with will flow from that person into the sick person upon contact. That anointing mixed with the faith of the sick person will drive out the sickness. It is important to understand that all believers can lay hands on the sick with the expectation that recovery and healing are imminent due to the indwelling, healing presence of the Holy Spirit.

Chapter Eight

POWERFUL HEALING TESTIMONIES

I T IS ALSO POSSIBLE TO minister healing to the sick through the laying on of hands with a tangible anointing of healing and miracle working power. This methodology is usually employed by those especially gifted and called to the healing ministry. The tangibility of the Spirit of God is one of the secrets of healing. The healing and miracle working power of God is capable of being touched, and it is perceptible to the touch. Not only is the healing power of God tangible, but it is also transferable. In Acts 19:11–12 one can read, "And God wrought special miracles by the hands of Paul: So that from his body were brought unto the sick handkerchiefs or aprons, and the diseases departed from them, and evil spirits went out of them."

Paul was given a special ministry of laying on of hands, and when he laid his hands on handkerchiefs and aprons, the anointing he was anointed with flowed into them, turning them into spiritual storage batteries, so to speak, of Holy Spirit miracle working power. When they were laid on the sick, they surcharged the body and healing was the result. People receive various levels of healing through this method because obtaining healing when exposed to God's tangible healing, and miracle working power is by degree, based on two conditions:

1. The degree of healing power administered, and
2. The degree of faith that gives action to that power.

In most cases, the sick person's faith must be combined with the healing power of God in order to get results when this method is used.

A few years ago, I was ministering in a church in Ohio speaking for a few days. There was a married couple from the church who were friends of mine. The husband, whom I will call Bob, was concerned about his parents who were aging and had not made a commitment to Jesus Christ. They often promised to come to church for Sunday services, but when Sunday arrived they would never show up. In fact, his parents had not been to church, except for weddings and funerals for many years.

The Lord had been doing some unusual things in the services, and toward the end of one of the services I invited anyone who knew someone who was ill but not in attendance to come forward and bring a handkerchief so that I could lay hands on it and anoint it with oil. Several people came and brought handkerchiefs. My married friends came forward as well. I laid hands on the handkerchiefs and prayed over them anointing them with oil.

What happened next was truly amazing. I didn't find out about it until much later. But, Bob told me that the Lord spoke to him and told him to give the handkerchief to his parents. The Lord also gave him explicit instructions not to let anyone else touch the handkerchief before he gave it to them. He said he put the handkerchief in a safe place overnight and gave instructions that no one was to touch it.

The next day he went to his parent's house and took the handkerchief with him. After having a conversation and spending time with them, just before leaving he handed the handkerchief to his father and told him, "Dad because you are the man of this house I am giving this to you. I believe the Lord wants me to give it to you." His father took it. Then Bob said, "See ya in church Sunday?" His father said they would be there. He had said this many times before only to renege when the actual time came.

When Sunday arrived, Bob and his wife were hopeful, but had been let down so many times, they just weren't sure what to expect. When the service started his parents were not there. But after a short while they showed up, came into the sanctuary and sat way in the back. After the sermon, an invitation was given to come forward to make a commitment to Christ. Bob's parents didn't move. And Bob began to pray, "Lord, it's been years since my parents have been in a church service. If you don't do something now, they may never make it back to church again." He said he no sooner got the words out of his mouth when his parents got up out of their seats and walked down to the front to receive Christ.

The following is an excerpt from a report written by the late Rev. Kenneth R. Tippin, former Church of God pastor in Marshall, Michigan. The following testimonials are put forth as examples of the ministry of laying on of hands in conjunction with a tangible anointing of healing and miracle working power.

The year was 1998 as Rev. Tippin recalls, "God is a mighty God! He is real and does answer prayer!! My feet are straightening out!!! They have been crooked for many years. The pain is minimal. I can go up the porch stairs at my daughter's house without holding on to the door knob. I have never been able to do this. I thank you Jesus. This is the testimony of healing of a member of the Church of God in Sturgis, Donelda Hart, who had crooked feet for many years and walked with a walker or cane. She has not used her walker or cane since November 8, 1998, the night of the divine healing service at Community Church of God in Marshall. Rev. Elliot Foggs (son of the General Secretary of the Church of God) came to share the ministry of healing. With him were his wife, two sons, his niece, cousin Jay (an elder at Sherman Street Church of God), Tyron Vertner, and George Pearson."

Pastor Tippin continued, "Our Sunday morning service had our best attendance of the year, even better than Easter. People came expecting to be blessed and brought their relatives. I rejoiced over three people for whom I was praying. I was hoping they would live until November 8 to be able to attend. In the morning service, his message was well received. He invited people who wanted ministry for healing to line up. A long line was formed. One of the church's board members was instantaneously healed of back pain. Another woman who is on oxygen for her heart condition felt incredible warmth tingling within her chest. She started breathing better. One woman noticed as she was leaving the church that her toe no longer hurt. It had been in severe pain for some time. Another woman, who was diagnosed with severe bipolar disorder, left feeling much better.

Pastor Tippin noted, "One of the incredible things to me was the positive response of the elderly long term members of our church. They were filled with joy and returned to the evening service. Some of them rarely come to a church activity at night. They arrived early and were anxiously awaiting to be blessed of the Lord! We invited our neighboring Church of God congregations to attend. In the evening cars began to fill our huge field out back. The sanctuary was nearly full by 5:30p.m. When the service began at 6p.m., the building was fuller than it had been in its' twenty year history. Extra chairs were lined down the middle aisle and the side aisles. We put extra chairs in the narthex and on the front platform.

Ministers that were seated on the platform included, Sister Lorraine Bolley, Rev. Paul Bickel, Rev. Doug Carr, Rev. Tim Kumpfer, Rev. Dean Carmoney, Rev. Henry Schwartz, Rev. Pete Clutter, Rev. Wayne Warner, Rev. John Mellish, Rev. Jerry Johnson, Rev. Ken Wiedrick, and also Brother Jerry Pettit (who pastors an independent church, but fellowships with our Battle Creek area CHOG ministers). Rev. Rick Webb was at the piano and led worship. The atmosphere was electric! The worship was enthusiastically glorious. Rev. Foggs preached a sermon that was well received. He invited people to line up for ministry. Pastors were invited to stand with parishioners as they received ministry and that was very precious. Following the time of ministry, a woman from the Sturgis church shared about the healing of her neck, which felt so good after a lengthy time of pain. Pastor Bickle of the Church of God at Burlington, Michigan also testified about healing in his right arm.

There were some who prayed for forgiveness of sins. It was very encouraging. Many of our people had never seen anything exactly like this fashion of a healing ministry in person. Rick Webb, who was at the piano, shared that as he watched the congregation many had eyes as large as saucers as they watched what was taking place. Yet the people kept coming. Dr. Keith Papendick, a physician from Minges Hills Church of God, shared what happened after he was seated for the service. 'I sat down and immediately had a severe and nearly debilitating spasm in my back.

I know very well that the prince of darkness was involved. I fought the pain. Since that night, my back has been better than it's been in a long time. Satan wanted me out of that room, and I believe the Lord rewarded my perseverance. I have been plagued with a bum arm for some time now, and it has been very sore, cold and achy for some time. A friend of mine told me I needed to see a hand surgeon, and let him have a look at it. Since hearing the message Sunday, I have had no ache, pain or severe coldness to my two outer fingers on my left hand . . . You see, anyone, literally everyone, who touched two of my fingers would have thought I was dead, while the remaining fingers were consistently normal. Since Sunday night, all my fingers have been normal. It is as if nothing was ever wrong with them.'

Juanita Lape, an elderly woman from the Grass Lake Church of God said, 'I had been suffering with arthritis so long and a stiff neck for a while, but as the preacher took hold of my head, a warm feeling came over me and felt like someone put an arm around me . . . . Praise the Lord! I ended up on the floor, and when I came to, my pain had become less and I had no stiff neck. They helped me up, and I walked away by myself without the fear of falling. Praise the Lord, I am healed.

Pastor Dean Carmoney of the Grass Lake Church of God reported that he held a testimony service a week later, November 15, in the morning service. He never got a chance to preach. The altars were filled over and over as people repented and presented themselves to God for healing and help. He believed the complete effects of the healing service have not begun to be felt.

In that November 15 testimony service, Judy Miller, who was born with hearing problems, who went through school lip reading, and who had worn hearing aids more than 30 years, went forward to pray. She says, 'At first I went up to the altar for my granddaughter who has a cold and is three years old. We were all praying for her. After that Pastor Dean laid his hands on my head. He was praying for several different things. It got real warm. He asked me to remove my hearing aids. He took his hands from my head and put them over my ears. Other people were praying for me and laying hands on me.

My ears became really hot. I felt an uncontrollable drone of vibration, a powerful penetration of heat way deep inside through my spine and my body, through my ears. It's something you never experienced before. Magnificent! I had a lot of peace and a lot of Joy. I could hear everybody and Pastor Dean. Now I can hear things without my hearing aids—my grandkids, the microwave, the telephone, high pitched sounds. I am overwhelmed and real content. It's unlike anything you ever experienced . . .'

One of the other reports from that service was a man who had smoked for more than 20 years, and after prayer no longer had the desire. He threw a pack of cigarettes away that night. Two weeks passed before he reported to the pastor he hadn't smoked since the service. He was used to smoking a pack-a-day. His smoking habit was so engrained that he told of continuing to reach into his upper shirt pocket periodically for the cigarettes, but then remembered he had quit. They were gone. He no longer had a physical desire for them, nor any withdrawal symptoms."

While visiting First Church of God in Columbus, Ohio, pastored by Bishop Timothy J. Clarke, I entered the sanctuary on a Wednesday night for their midweek service. I had no ministerial responsibilities, so I just went in and found a seat. Suddenly four or five rows behind me there was a stir. I heard someone saying, "That's him! That's him! That's him!" Not sure about whom they were speaking, or what exactly was going on I remained in my seat and waited for the service to begin. However, as the commotion behind me got louder and louder, I finally turned completely around to see what was happening. When I did, a lady said excitedly, "I told you that was him!" She then came up to me with her friend and apologized for being so exuberant. Then she began to share her story.

I had been to the church two years earlier and had conducted a healing service. During the service, the tangible healing and miracle working power of God were in operation. I prayed for many. This woman had kidney failure and was one of the ones I had laid hands on during the meeting. She said to me, "You healed my kidneys." I said, "God did it." She then said, "Yea, but he used you to do it." Then she told me that she had been on dialysis and that her kidneys were failing. She was on the list for a kidney transplant. After prayer, however, she went back to the doctor. They examined her kidneys and told her there was nothing wrong with them. Her kidneys were like new—perfect. Even the doctor said it was a miracle.

At Jubilee Christian Church under the leadership of Bishop G. A. Thompson, I was informed about a young man who had difficulty hearing and wore hearing aids. He was instantly healed during one of the services while the tangible healing and miracle working power of God were present. He no longer required hearing aids. Another woman at Anderson Campmeeting born deaf in one ear had her ear opened, her hearing restored, and the Lord instantly healed her for the first time in her life during one of our healing services.

But the question has been asked, and legitimately so. Were these people actually healed? Are these stories true?

Well, if they are true for no one else, they are true for those whose lives were affected by the tangible healing and miracle working power of God. Their families, churches and all who know their stories bear witness to the mercy and grace of God, who has chosen to reveal Himself to us in this way. Where we can, now we are getting medical corroboration. Laying on of hands with a tangible anointing of healing and miracle working power can be a potent source of healing. It can bring relief to many who suffer with various diseases and conditions for which medical science at present has no answer. To God be the glory!

Chapter Nine

ANOINTING AND AGREEMENT IN PRAYER

JAMES 5:14-15 SAYS, "IS ANY sick among you? Let him call for the elders of the church; and let them pray over him, anointing him with oil in the name of the Lord: And the prayer of faith shall save the sick, and the Lord shall raise him up; and if he has committed sins, they shall be forgiven him."

Anointing with oil is another method whereby healing can be obtained through the Word of God. Thankfully this method is still widely used throughout much of the church world today. In the scriptures oil has been symbolic and representative of the Holy Spirit. It has also been known to have properties useful to healing when combined with prayer. Notice the scripture says to call for the elders of the church. It is the responsibility of the sick person to call. One should not complain because no one has come to visit during a time of illness. Call for the elders! Let them pray and anoint with oil. The promise of God is, "The prayer of faith will save (restore/heal) the sick, and the Lord shall raise him up." If we will do what God said to do and believe His words, we will get the results He promised. Praise God, there is no failure in God's word!

Early in the ministry of the disciples Jesus had taught them that the anointing with oil would be a significant part of their ministry to the hurting masses. It is recorded in the book of Mark that the disciples being dispatched by Jesus into the then known world, ". . . cast out many devils, and anointed many with oil, and healed them" (Mark 6:13). Anointing with oil for healing was a part of the Apostle's training for ministry.

Jesus makes another profound statement in Matthew 18:19–20. He says, "Again I say unto you. That if two of you agree on earth as touching anything that they shall ask, it shall be done for them of my father which is in heaven. For wherever two or three are gathered together in my name, there am I in the midst of them." The importance of agreement cannot be over emphasized. Jesus promised that where two were in agreement, asking in his name, whatever the request it would be done. Our agreement affects and activates heaven. God moves when He sees agreement.

It is important to understand that the good things promised in scripture, like healing, don't automatically come our way because of a personal relationship with Jesus Christ. There are many reasons it is often a struggle to receive healing. Primarily, there are evil forces in the world determined to keep people from ever receiving what God has declared is rightfully theirs. When it comes to healing, people are often required to do something in order to receive the healing.

Someone may ask, well if God wants us to be healed then why doesn't He just heal everybody? The same question could be asked in regards to salvation. People must do something to receive the gift of salvation. In like manner, often people must do something to be healed. In the Old Testament, Naaman the leper was required to go wash in the Jordan river before his healing was manifested, and not just once, but seven times (2 Kings 5:9-10). If he had refused, he would have undoubtedly been a leper until the day of his death. In the New Testament Jesus heals a blind man, but as a part of the process, he gives him explicit instructions to, "Go wash in the pool of Siloam" (John 9:5-7). As he did what Jesus commanded, his sight was restored. Obedience to God's explicit instructions is a major key to receiving our healing and getting in agreement with someone else about our healing will bring powerful results.

When we agree on earth as the scripture says, Jesus, himself, enters into the agreement with us. In many churches, the scripture found in Matthew 18:20 is used to refer to a church service, and it is true the Lord is there. But the scripture is actually talking about wherever there are two people agreeing. They could be in an office building, talking to one another on the telephone, in an automobile, on the street or flying together on an airplane. Wherever they are, if they will get into agreement on something that the Bible promises, then Jesus says he will enter into that agreement and the Father will cause what they've asked to come to pass. Actually the Father does the work as if He is doing it for Jesus, because He is.

In one particular case, a woman in California (we'll call her Constance) had been suffering with a rare blood disease for many years. Over the years, she had two blood transfusions to try to fix the problem. And she was scheduled to go back to the hospital for another transfusion. All of this was revealed to me by my mother-in-law the night before the scheduled procedure. Mom asked if I would call Constance and pray with her. At first, I really didn't want to because I assumed Constance wouldn't understand what I was doing. And I didn't want her to think I was trying to force something on her. I had no knowledge of her spiritual life or what she believed about God or the Bible. But my mother-in-law prevailed.

When I called Constance, we talked for a while, and I shared with her that my mother-in-law informed me she was scheduled for a blood transfusion the following day. After she described her situation to me, I asked if she would mind if we prayed. She said it was okay for me to pray. So we prayed together that God would heal her of her blood disease. It was a very simple prayer. And I thought from her response that she wasn't really tracking with me. But, the next day I got a phone call from Constance. She said she went to see the doctor as scheduled. During her preparation for the transfusion, they ran some preliminary blood tests.

She said the doctor came back into her room with a look of disbelief and bewilderment on his face. He then asked what she had been doing. She said she hadn't done anything unusual, or different. She had done nothing outside of her normal routine. Then he told her that her blood tested completely normal. He said it was impossible for her blood condition to change overnight as it had. He continued saying there was no need for a blood transfusion, but that they wanted to keep her on her medication and watch her. She said the doctor just kept shaking his head in amazement saying, "This is impossible." Well, with men it is impossible, but not with God. For with God nothing shall be impossible! The prayer of agreement can produce stellar healing results.

Chapter Ten

GIFTS FROM THE HAND OF GOD

NOW GIFTS OF THE SPIRIT are manifestations of the Holy Spirit. They can bring healing to a person's body, and they are manifested in various ways. In 1 Corinthians 12:4-11 one can read, "Now there are diversities of gifts, but the same Spirit. And there are differences of administrations, but the same Lord. And there are diversities of operations, but it is the same God which worketh all in all. But the manifestation of the Spirit is given to every man to profit withal. For to one is given by the Spirit the word of wisdom; to another the word of knowledge by the same Spirit. To another faith by the same Spirit to another the gifts of healing by the same Spirit, to another the working of miracles; to another prophecy; to another discerning of spirits, to another divers kinds of tongues; to another the interpretation of tongues: But all these worketh that one and selfsame Spirit, dividing to every man severally as He will."

Through gifts of the Spirit, healing generally takes little or no faith at all on the part of the sick person. It goes beyond all human understanding and comprehension and operates as a divine, sovereign act of God. No person of his own will can produce the gifts of the Spirit. They originate with God alone. They are initiated by Him, controlled by Him and manifested in accordance with His own divine purpose and will. An example would be the instance in the book of Acts where the shadow of Peter was used by God as an instrument to heal the sick. (Acts 5:14-16) That part of Peter's ministry could be categorized as the working of special miracles. In Acts 19:11 the Apostle Paul experiences a similar manifestation of spiritual power and supernatural healing through handkerchiefs and aprons. The primary gifts of the Spirit used in healing are:

1. The word of knowledge
2. The gift of special faith
3. The gifts of healing
4. The working of miracles
5. The discerning of spirits

One may see a combination of these gifts and methods working together to bring healing to a person.

Several years ago I conducted a healing meeting at Power Centre Church, International in Bellville, Michigan. The pastor at the time was Apostle Rita J. Johnson. As I was waiting in the Pastor's office for the worship service to begin, a few of the church members came into the office and began to tell me a story about a little seven-year-old girl who was going to be in the service that night who had been diagnosed with cancer of the blood and bones. She was taking nine different medications, and it was reported to me that the medications the doctors were giving her were not working. Medical science had basically given her up to die. I was also informed that the doctors said a bone marrow transplant might extend her life, but would not save her. Due to her dire condition, the Make-A-Wish Foundation had given her and her family an all-expense paid trip to Disney World. Then they told me her mother wanted me to pray for the child while I was there. I said I would pray for her, and then they left the office.

When conducting a meeting like this, there is such a focus on preparation to be a channel for the Holy Spirit, I paid little attention to what was said, but rather honed in on the meeting at hand. Soon the time for service to begin arrived. There was singing and worship. Then it was time to deliver the message. I taught on one of the principles of healing for about an hour. After which I asked if anyone wanted to come forward to receive healing prayer combined with the laying on of hands.

Several people came forward for prayer that night. So I began laying hands on each one of them, one by one. After I had prayed for nearly half the line, I saw out of the corner of my eye a little girl being carried by a woman, who I later discovered was the little girl's mother. She was getting into the line. Then someone came up behind me and whispered in my ear, "That's the little girl we were telling you about." I never turned around to see who was talking to me. I kept praying for those in the line, and when the woman and child got three or four yards away from me, the Spirit of God came upon me and I stopped praying for those in the line, turned and pointed to the little girl and said, "You don't need a bone marrow transplant, you're healed." I didn't say any more than that. The mother had a look of incredulity. And I later found out she was somewhat upset with me because I didn't pray for her child, lay hands on her, or anoint her with oil. She returned to her seat. And after some time everyone who had come forward for prayer had been prayed for, and the service was dismissed.

The next day I drove back home and nearly two weeks later I called the church to talk with Apostle Johnson about an unrelated matter. After talking a while, I asked, "By the way, what happened to the little girl?" The pastor said, "You haven't heard?" I said that I hadn't. Then she told me the story that the mother had taken the girl back to the doctor and the doctor asked the mother what she had been doing. The mother said she hadn't been doing anything different. Then the doctor said, "You've been doing something because your daughter's blood is changing. She doesn't need a bone marrow transplant right now, but we want to keep an eye on her because something is happening with her blood." The mother maintained that she had done nothing new or different. The doctor said there was no way her blood could just change like that.

After a few weeks, the little girl was declared well and taken off of all her medications. Several years later I went back to Bellville to interview the girl, her mother and aunt. Eight years had actually passed since the healing service, and she was fifteen years old at the time of the interview.

She was on the girl's basketball team at her school and was in the band playing the saxophone. Since the age of seven she had an annual check-up. No trace of the disease was ever found again.

In this case, the healing was not done by my will or my intention, but by a sovereign act of God, using me as the channel or conduit through which healing and miracle working power passed to bring healing to the life of someone for whom medical science had no answer. It was a combination of the gift of special faith, the word of knowledge and gifts of healing. Scripture informs us that these gifts can be administered differently. They may also operate differently. In other words, the same gift doesn't always operate the same way. And similar gifts may operate differently in different people. The Holy Spirit is the director in administering the gifts of the Spirit.

When the gifts of the Spirit are in operation, it is imperative that we follow the lead of the Holy Spirit. It cannot be over emphasized that these gifts are manifested by His will alone. We have found that when anyone is moving in a so-called gift with selfish or purely profit motive, or they appear to be controlling the gift, or operating these gifts at will, this can be an open door for the operation of evil spirits, familiar spirits who are also seeking expression in the physical world. One thing we need most is the ability to discern what spirit is in operation. If it is truly the Holy Spirit, God and Jesus Christ will be glorified, and the result is a blessing for all involved. One will tend to see the glorification of individuals and personalities when less than pure spirits are in operation. The scripture implores, "Beloved, believe not every spirit, but test the spirits to see whether they be of God: Because many false prophets have gone out into the world." (1 John 4:1) To examine additional scriptural applications of these principles read Mark chapters 7 and 8; John 9:1-7; Proverbs 4:20; Isaiah 6:9-10; Matthew 13:14-15; and Psalms 107:20.

Chapter Eleven

HEALING AND THE INEVITABILITY OF DEATH

SOME MAY WONDER, WHAT IS the purpose of this healing business? After all, in the end we all die. And who can deny the interconnection between sickness and death? We all know someone who was sick and subsequently died of his illness. The scriptures declare, "It is appointed unto men once to die and after this the judgment" (Hebrews 9:27).

A lady came up to me one time after a healing meeting and asked, "Have any of the people you have prayed for died?" I answered, "All of the people that I pray for die." I continued, "That puts me in pretty good company because everyone that Jesus ministered to died, and all who were healed by the apostles also died." There is no flesh and blood person walking around for 2000 years. All from Jesus' day are dead.

What the woman was really asking me was, is your healing ministry authentic—does it work, do people really get healed? The short answer is yes; people do get healed, but those same people sooner or later inevitably die. And sadly very often people can lose their healing. Both 1 Thessalonians 5:21 and Revelations 3:11 forewarn us to hold fast to the good things we have received from the Lord because we have an enemy who is out to kill, steal and destroy.

There are three primary reasons why Christians and others are not healed. Those same three reasons account for why many lose their healing. First, many have no idea that healing belongs to them scripturally. They have not been taught the truth of God's word on the subject. Second, those who may know what belongs to them are often weak in faith, so they either never receive healing, or lose it some time after they are initially healed. And finally, sometimes people are living in disobedience to the known will of God, which is what gave sickness access to mankind in the beginning.

God's healing and miracle working power can heal any malady, prolong natural life and delay physical death caused by disease. In fact, healing for the physical body when understood in its proper biblical context is a by-product of eternal life that begins in the life of a follower of Jesus Christ on earth, not in heaven. True death is separation from all of the good that God is—all he possesses—his loving kindness, his tender mercies, his compassions, his truth, and from his grace and divine influence upon the life. Death is the anticipation of an engagement with God's wrath. It is all-consuming. Death encompasses far more and is infinitely more devastating than the demise of physical life. It is the place of outer darkness where no light appears, where sorrows immeasurable abound. When one focuses entirely and merely on physical death in relation to healing, one does a disservice to any address of the subject.

How, one may ask if God is omnipresent, could someone be separated from Him? Quite simply, through His might, His omnipotence, He has the ability to separate Himself from whom He will, as well as unite Himself with whom He will. And as scripture affirms, those who know not Christ are dead already even though they still have a physical existence (Ephesians 2:1). They are just not conscious of their death state. Unfortunately, many are blinded and will not become aware of their death state until physical death occurs, at which point the death state is locked in, irreversible.

Death is much more about location, relationship, condition of the human spirit, and final abode than it is about the ending of physical life. Is one in Christ? Does one have a relationship with God? Has one's spirit been reborn? And is one destined for heaven? The answers to these questions reveal a person's state whether alive physically or dead physically. Answer each of these questions for oneself incorrectly and one is in the grips of death even while living. Answer each correctly and one is alive forevermore, even in the face and onslaught of physical death. Jesus boldly declared on the way to Lazarus' tomb, "I am the resurrection and the life: he that believeth on me, though he were dead yet shall he live: and whosoever liveth and believeth on me shall never die" (John 11:25-26). Physical death could be described as a transition, a graduation of being. What we go through this life becoming, finally in fullness at physical death we become.

Healing, on the other hand, is a representation of the will of God on earth. Prayer for healing, one author has written, is not overcoming God's reluctance, but rather it is laying hold to his highest willingness. Healing is the ushering in of the Kingdom of God into a dark world. When Jesus taught his disciples to pray he instructed them to say, "Thy kingdom come, thy will be done on earth as it is in heaven" (Matthew 6:10). Then he commanded them to go out and heal the sick, raise the dead, and cleanse the lepers. One must understand there is no sickness in heaven, disease, pain or suffering. When we work to bring healing to earth we are acting in a high order of God's divine purpose and will.

But someone may say, yes, but doesn't a person have to get sick to die? We all have to die of something, right? And isn't the wearing out of the physical body due to use a sign of disease? Certainly disease often is responsible for physical death along with accidents. That's undeniable. A few months ago, when my niece was tragically killed in an automobile accident at the age of 21 it was difficult to detect any purpose in such an event. Where was God in all of it? Why didn't He spare her life? Many other questions arose. And although I know she is gone on to heaven, there remains a cloak of mystery around the event that I suspect will not be completely unveiled in this life. So, there are mysteries, and there are situations that we don't understand.

But God's word makes clear statements about healing from disease. One dictionary definition states that in an organism, a disease may be defined as an abnormal condition, one that produces specific signs or symptoms (http://en.wikipedia.org/wiki/Disease). Consider the words, abnormal condition, in the above definition. For illustrative purposes, when a light bulb burns out in the family room or kitchen, do we consider that an abnormal event? No, it is quite normal. In fact, we know and fully expect that the bulb will go out in time, not because of any defect but because it only has a limited life expectancy. The light will not burn out until it has finished its purpose. We actually have additional light bulbs in the closet or cabinet prepared for such an eventuality. We count it a normal, expected occurrence that light bulbs will burn out.

Now if we purchased light bulbs and they burned out after only two days use, we would know there was a problem. That would be abnormal. A light bulb burning out over a reasonable period is very normal. We should no more consider the wearing out of the body in old age an abnormal condition, i.e. a disease, any more than we would view a burned out light bulb as an abnormality. Light bulbs eventually burn out. It is unavoidable, inevitable, just as death. Light bulbs, batteries, appliances and the like all have life expectancy.

God has given mankind life expectancy of 70 to 80 years or more (Psalms 90:10). God makes a statement in Genesis that man's days will be 120 years (Genesis 6:3). But no matter how long we live death is a normal part of life. Now technology is producing light bulbs and batteries that last longer. Medical science is making discoveries that aid people in living longer. But even with all of the modern advances, if the Lord tarries, we shall certainly all succumb. Death's tragedy, however, is not the demise of the physical body, but rather it is in one's being out of position when it occurs, i.e., not being in Christ.

When the coroner confirms on a death certificate a person has died of natural causes, medically speaking, any number of diseases, or no disease could be identified as the culprit. And old age is not a scientifically recognized cause of death. So, whether one has to be sick to die, in a technical sense, remains a question for physicians and the medical community, because much of our understanding of death in Western culture today is based on the knowledge we have gained from modern medical science. And descriptions of death commonly used in society often are couched in technical medical language that has been disseminated throughout the culture by the medical community.

However, the scriptures are clear. There is no scripture suggesting one must be sick to die. In fact, scripture seems to imply the opposite. In the Old Testament if one looks at the lives of Abraham, Isaac, Jacob, Joseph, Moses, Joshua, and David among many others, the overwhelming pattern is these men lived till old age. Many lived 100 years or more and then died with no inference to sickness or disease being the cause of their deaths. This is significant because the Bible is replete with instances of various people experiencing death attributed to sickness or accidents, from those in Pharaoh's regime pre-Exodus, to various ones of the children of Israel. One instance deserving special note is the death of Asa king of Judah. In the book of 1 Chronicles 16:12-14 the scripture records, "And Asa in the thirty and ninth year of his reign was diseased in his feet, until his disease was exceeding great: yet in his disease he sought not the Lord, but to the physicians. And Asa slept with his fathers, and died in the one and fortieth year of his reign." Asa was sick for two years getting progressively worse until he died.

In Leviticus chapter 13, leprosy is addressed, and the priesthood is given specific instructions on how to deal with the disease. In the Old Testament, disease seemed more pronounced and was amplified as a judgment rendered for disobedience to God. It is clear that disease was a recognized part of Old Testament culture. The scripture does not hide from its reality and neither should we. Sickness and disease do not affect the character of God at all, but in scripture disease provides an opportunity for God to reveal himself to mankind as a beneficent healer (Exodus 15:26).

Those with a faith in Jesus Christ go through, rather than to sickness, like a running-back running through a would-be tackler in a football game. Sickness is not intended to be the final stop on this journey called life. The only death recorded among believers attributed to sickness in the New Testament after Jesus' resurrection is that of Dorcus or Tabitha (Acts 9:36-41). And after she dies, the church calls for Peter to come, who upon arriving through prayer ends up raising her from the dead. At that point, she is also made completely well. If healing had not come after being raised from the dead, Dorcus certainly would have shortly succumbed to her illness again.

Today many modes of death exist. But in the beginning it was not so. Death was not a part of God's original plan. He who created the earth and everything in it said His creation was good. Death entered as a result of sin. I, therefore, submit for your consideration that it is not imperative to believe, as much of Western culture does; that sickness and disease are or must be the dominant agency for the facilitation of physical death. Is it possible to transition from this life with out exiting through the door of illness? Wouldn't a good goal be to leave this physical existence well in body, mind, and spirit at a ripe old age?

Ultimately, shouldn't one at least be able to live long enough to fulfill the divine purpose and will for which one was created? To complete the assignment one has been given, to be a father, mother, grand parent, doctor, lawyer, public servant, school teacher, minister, laborer, administrator, philanthropist, or any number of other positions or occupations? Whatever one's station in life, at all times and in all ways, in particular when death threatens to terminate prematurely one's purpose and divine assignment, sickness should be vehemently opposed and resisted. Also, it will help to remember that death in all its facets is an enemy of God (1 Corinthians 15:26). This is a great mystery, but why would one not resist the enemy of one's Master and Lord? To be sure there are unseen forces at work causing the spread of disease in the earth with death as the desired outcome, but through faith the believer in Jesus Christ has a unique advantage.

As was mentioned earlier, there is still the mystery of innocent babies and small children with atrocious sicknesses and ravaging diseases, as well as others born with crippling conditions and those who suffer life–altering, deforming accidents. Stories revealing these conditions can be heart wrenching and cause one to ask many questions. But the job at hand is to minister healing to all we can, knowing that the infinite and all–wise God is not impeded at all by any human malady and He looks for us to put our trust in Him. Because miracles of healing are always possible, and hope for healing is never out of order.

Finally, let us recall the words spoken by the Holy Spirit through the Psalmist David, "Because he has set his love upon me, therefore, will I deliver him. I will set him on high because he has known My name. He shall call upon Me and I will answer him. I will be with him in trouble. I will deliver him and honor him. With *long life* will I satisfy him and show him My salvation" (Psalms 91:14–16). In light of the scripture, it might serve one well to ask a different question. Instead of asking must one be sick to die, perhaps the better question may be, is healing God's will for us? And if so, are we open right now to accepting our healing from the hand of a gracious God?

Chapter Twelve

THE QUEST FOR SOLUTIONS

O NE HOT, SUNNY AFTERNOON IN August as I sat in my home study in prayer and meditation, I began thinking about all of the healing experiences I had over the years. The primary event that began formulating in my mind was the time in Michigan where the little girl I mentioned earlier in chapter 10, given up to die by medical science had been cured of cancer and a rare blood disease. The Make-A-Wish Foundation had given her, and her family an all expense paid trip to Disney World. I became fixated on how it all appeared to have happened through simply speaking an anointed word.

Beginning to pray and commune with the Lord, I questioned, how can this type of healing be increased so that people experience more and more of it. Although thoroughly confident that I was not the healer, Jesus Christ is. I yet believed I had a responsibility before God to do everything in my power to bring healing to as many people as I could. There was no way I could reach all of the little girls like the one in Michigan even if I spent 24 hours a day, 7 days a week, 365 days a year conducting healing meetings. I did the math.

If I held two healing meetings every day for the next 30 years (highly improbable) with 1,000 people in attendance at each meeting, I would reach 21.9 million people directly, less than 1% of the earth's population. Then I thought maybe technology has something to offer. Suddenly, while meditating on these thoughts, I had a vision. With my eyes closed, I saw a small computer chip surrounded by what appeared to be a hazy cloud, which I perceived as the glory of God. The chip could be loaded with healing words that would speak audibly to the bodies of those suffering with sickness and disease. The thoughts were coming rapidly. Since the little girl had been healed in Michigan by just speaking a word, perhaps a computer chip with healing words on it could bring healing as well. The chip would work non-stop speaking healing words and delivering healing power to sick persons.

For the next several days, I mulled over these thoughts in my mind. I was excited about the prospect of a voice chip speaking continuous healing words and prayer to the body of someone who was ill. So, I contacted a major computer chip manufacturer in California. After signing non-disclosure documents I began revealing the concept. They gave me direction on technical aspects of creating such a device along with costs and production schedules, but it wasn't right. Something was missing.

Shortly after these things I began to assemble a team of professionals who could provide counsel for me as I explored how to bring this vision to life. I brought on Kenneth

Wilson, an entrepreneur with thirty years experience in marketing and advertising. Ken is the principal at a Southern California advertising agency. Gerald Edwards was added to the team next. With extensive manufacturing experience, Gerald was the owner of a plastics manufacturing operation that generated nearly $100 million in sales annually. And finally, we needed someone with a strong finance and investment background, so we added Joe McGuirl to the team. Joe had experience in patents, along with FDA procedures, requirements and rules for new drugs. He also had a comprehensive venture capital background and had generated millions of dollars for the research program of a prominent east coast university.

With the establishment of a solid team, we began holding weekly conference calls to hammer out all of the business and product development issues around creating what we were calling the Centurion Natural Order Device (CNOD). We developed a business plan and began the search for electronic devices already available in the market that would meet our exact requirements. Soon I came across the technology that seemed tailor made for our endeavor.

Next, I began creating what would come to be known as healing content. Our healing content was comprised of healing scripture—words from the Bible that addressed the subject of healing—along with specific disease state information and faith commands. In a production studio, I layered these elements onto an audio recording. Once the recording was created, I added another layer of nature sounds so the actual content could not be consciously detected.

Of course, this is not new. Subliminal messages, techniques and recordings have been around for many years. However, we do not look at our work primarily as subliminal, but rather spiritual. In fact, we have no interest in influencing a sick person's subconscious mind in any way, though that may be one affect. We instead are focused on reaching deep within the spiritual nature and makeup of humankind and attacking the disease at its base level, the spiritual level. With the CNOD, we are directing healing words and spiritual power to the root of the disease. And we believe that we can weaken, disable, and even destroy the spiritual support structure behind the disease through the use of anointed words.

Now, some have said to me, "Ed, what you're doing amounts to no more than placebo." When I hear those kinds of statements I wonder if these people have ever read the studies on the effectiveness of placebo. It is well documented that placebo can be powerful and at times even work as well as the actual drug being studied. But what we are doing goes beyond placebo. There is not one report of placebo healing a cancer-ridden deathly ill seven year old child, given up to die by medical science. Placebo has never been credited with healing the ears of an elderly person born deaf so that the person hears sounds for the first time in her life. If this is placebo, Lord, please give us more!

In order to protect the healing content from misuse, we hired a law firm to file for a provisional patent. Now healing content exists and is ready for use with a number of categorical disease states. And we have selected a manufacturer to produce MP3/4 devices for internal testing and prototype development.

Here is what we learned early on. First, the CNOD needed to be worn by study participants in an arm band that would allow for flexibility and care-free comfort. Second, active listening was not required or desirable for the healing content to be effective. And finally, we discovered a need to establish a time frame for participant exposure to the healing content—a dosage. The idea of prayer dosing of healing content has become one of the cornerstones of all CNOD use. We believe that the ability to successfully and accurately dose healing content by disease state has the potential to provide relief to persons suffering with disease worldwide. There will be profound implications when the healing content dosing theory is proven to be effective in clinical studies utilizing large numbers. Now we have the ability to conduct double-blind research to determine at which dosage and for which diseases healing content is most effective.

CONCLUSION

THE MOST IMPORTANT THING ONE should know about healing and sickness is that they are both spiritual. They have spiritual roots from which they develop and grow. The importance of these truths has to do with the fact that any time we attempt to solve spiritual problems like sickness with physical answers alone we fall short. This would explain in part the reason that although medical science has made significant advancements there yet remains much sickness and disease in the world. We must begin dealing with sickness from its root causes.

Now we can open our hearts and minds to an infinite Creator who can bring healing to our bodies, minds and emotions through a variety of ways, including modern medicine. Armed with this knowledge, there is never a reason to give up hope. Even when medical science has done its best and been unsuccessful, there remains through Christ the ability to obtain the healing we so earnestly desire. And through His Spirit, God provides various methods of healing to meet everyone on their individual level of faith.

HEALING PRAYER

Dear Heavenly Father,

I thank you and praise you for sending Jesus Christ to die on the cross for my sins. Thank you that because of his shed blood I can receive healing for my physical body. I now choose to believe that Jesus bore my sicknesses and diseases on the cross so that I could be free from sickness, disease and pain. I ask you to heal me now, Lord! And I thank you for providing healing for me. I receive my healing now in Jesus' name. AMEN.

PRAYER OF SALVATION

Jesus, I believe that you are Lord. Today I confess you as Lord of my life. I believe with all my heart that you died on the cross for my sins and that God raised you from the dead. I know that I have sinned and I am sorry for my sins. Forgive me and come into my heart Lord Jesus. Amen.

Appendix A

CNOD CASE STUDY

1. How Healing Prayer Content Reduced Disease Symptoms in 77% of Study Participants

1.1. Summary

In 2010 Centurion Bioenergy, LLC set out to conduct uncontrolled, experimental Complimentary and Alternative Medicine (CAM) trials on seven chronic disease states—cancer, asthma, hypertension, heart disease, long-term pain, arthritis, and depression. This on-going research is being funded by private investment. Our objective was to investigate whether masked, pre-recorded, continuous intercessory prayer played on an electronic MP3 device called Cnod™ and worn in an elastic band by the study participant would produce measurable improvements in the person's disease state. Also we wanted to learn what the most effective healing prayer dosage is for various chronic diseases. Two primary targets were chosen for the study, women between the ages of 22 and 54, and women age 55 to 85, clinically diagnosed with one or more of the selected chronic disease states. Men were allowed to participate by special request. Those selected for the study must believe that prayer helps, that healing miracles can occur today, and have a faith rating of at least 5 on a scale of 1 to 10. The study requires that each participant receive a continuous prayer dosage minimum of 120 hours during the 30-day trial period and file a weekly report. Because it is easiest to measure, our primary focus during this first phase of trials has been on pain reduction and elimination.

Results: 24 study participants—77% of study participants with chronic pain reported that their pain was reduced during the study period. Improvements ranged from complete pain elimination to 75% to 90% improvement over the study period. 100% of study participants suffering from chronic pain due to arthritis reported pain reduction. 38% of study participants reported having heightened feelings of happiness and peacefulness during the study period. They simply felt better. 38% of study participants purchased a Cnod™ at the end of the study period for their own continued personal use. Other interesting findings were that schizophrenia and depression were positively impacted as a result of continuous healing prayer electronically delivered through the Cnod™.

1.2. Trial Participant Profile

Women in our CAM trial were between the ages of 44 and 80, college educated, and had one of the seven chronic diseases, i.e., cancer, asthma, hypertension, heart disease, long-term pain, arthritis, or depression. The majority of study participants had a combination of chronic pain along with some other chronic condition, i.e., hypertension, depression, etc. All were on prescription medication. All had chronic disease symptoms in excess of two years. The primary method of trial participant recruitment was via television advertising on LeSea Broadcasting TV Network along with sphere of influence communication.

In a more comprehensive study conducted by the National Center for Health Statistics and the National Center for Complimentary and Alternative Medicine, it was found that healing prayer is the number one CAM therapy by far. And that 45% of all U.S. adults pray for healing, either for themselves or for others. This ground-breaking study of more than 30,000 adults also identified the majority of healing prayer users as female, between the ages of 22 and 54, college educated, with some type of chronic physical ailment, thus the selection of our target group.

2. Problem

2.1. Context

How can intercessory prayer be leveraged in the medical community to take advantage of its long-standing acceptance and effectiveness? How can intercessory prayer products be developed, branded, and brought to market?

More than 23 controlled medical research studies involving 2,774 persons have been conducted on the power of intercessory prayer. 57% of the studies indicated that prayer for healing had a definite and positive influence on health outcomes. 39% of studies showed no apparent effect. 4% of studies produced a negative outcome, according to E. Ernst's Systematic Review of the Data. Three major challenges with all of the previous studies were, 1) There was no way to know the proper prayer "dose" for maximum effectiveness, 2) There was no way to mitigate the effects of "background prayer", i.e., prayer from family and friends that could conceivably skew the study, and 3) There was no real way to establish, nor any mode for comprehending pray-er effectiveness. Centurion Bioenergy is developing healing prayer methodologies and techniques through the Cnod™ that are effective, repeatable, and predictable.

Medical science as a whole has been reluctant to openly validate healing prayer, or incorporate it into its daily practice. Unlike new "miracle drugs", there are no giant corporations, responsible to boards and Wall Street, behind healing prayer selling it to the medical community. And unlike new medical procedures, and devices, there is no profit motive for making healing prayer an integral part of the daily practice of medicine, and yet it is used by more than 100 million Americans to improve health. With the advent of the Cnod™, classified as a para-medical device, a business model now exists that can help establish healing prayer as an easily accessible tool physicians and medical professionals can use for the health and well being of their patients.

2.2. Objectives

The challenge was to create a spiritual, intercessory prayer device that would offer a recommended daily dosage of continuous healing prayer to those wishing to capitalize on the time-tested power of prayer. The solution would need to be non-intrusive, allowing the study participants to wear the device without having to change their daily routine. It would need to be reliable, flexible and have high durability. Cnod™ MP3/4 technologies were selected over several alternatives because of these requirements. Next was to test what effect 120 hours of continuous healing prayer would have on various disease states by recruiting a minimum of 10 study participants who have disease states falling within predetermined categories.

To assist with product development, we secured the resources of Azmuth Recording Studio. Their expertise enabled us to create a pristine product with excellent sound quality.

3. Solution

3.1. Process

1. We selected a manufacturing company in China to produce the Cnod™ units we would utilize.

2. We created the healing content and hired Azmuth Recording Studio to handle recording and all audio production of the healing prayer content and its masking,

then hired a patent law firm to file for a provisional patent for the content and processes we had developed.

3. We set up a production center and warehouse in Ann Arbor, Michigan where healing prayer content would be downloaded onto the Cnod™. The production center would also provide inventory management and product quality control.

4. We selected 7 chronic disease categories.

5. We determined the length of the study to be 30 days per participant and the daily healing prayer dosage to be 4 hours per day—2 hours in the morning and 2 hours in the evening based on available technology. This would give each participant a total of 120 hours of continuous healing prayer over the 30 day period.

6. We hired ICAN Advertising Agency to create advertising we could use to recruit study participants. The agency created a 30-second TV commercial, and collateral materials for recruitment purposes.

7. We selected the study design, which included an initial telephone qualification, health survey interview, approval by participants of an informed consent document, shipping of a Cnod™ healing prayer device to study participants, the completion of a weekly questionnaire, and an exit interview at the end of the study.

8. We ran direct response ads on Le Sea Broadcasting TV Network with an 800 number and distributed collateral materials to appropriate venues to recruit study participants. We invested in television airtime to discover when the best time would be for our target market to see our recruitment advertising.

9. We responded to inquires from prospective study participants, conducted necessary interviews with them and enrolled qualified candidates into the study. Within the first 8 hours of continuous healing prayer 38% of the study participants began experiencing heightened feelings of happiness, peace and general well being. There was increased expectation and anticipation of improved health with hopefulness. We found that in as few as 12 hours of continuous healing prayer some participants began to notice changes in their disease symptoms. Long-standing, stubborn symptoms began to dissipate. By between 56 and 84 hours most study participants had acknowledged a reduction in pain, or some other significant physiological change in their condition, i.e., no more inflammation in hands and joints. Some changes in symptoms were subtle, gradual, and some were dramatic.

10. We addressed equipment failure issues by swapping out Cnod™ units when necessary.

3.2. Technologies and Delivery Method

The Cnod™ is a 1GB electronic device utilizing MP3/4 technology, with an external speaker. It hosts pre-recorded healing prayer content that plays in a loop via a repeater function. The Cnod™ is worn in an elastic band around the study participant's arm or leg releasing continuous, masked healing prayer and spiritual power into the molecular structure of the person's physiology and into their spirit. Because of the short 2.5 to 3 hour battery life of the units, for the study we recommended 4 hours of use per day in 2-hour intervals. This would give the user the ability to wear the device for 2 hours, recharge the battery, and wear it for an additional 2 hours at another time that day. The Cnod™ will make prayer research more reliable, and more accessible to physicians and medical practitioners.

3.3. Conclusion

Close proximity, electronically delivered intercessory prayer was associated with lower pain scores, overall feelings of happiness, peacefulness and general wellbeing. This result suggests that close proximity, electronically delivered, intercessory prayer may be an effective adjunct to standard medical care.

Janet—IN

Janet is a housewife, mother and grandmother, who had severe pain in the knees, shoulder and neck due to arthritis. The condition began more than a year ago. The pain in her knees was so acute that it was debilitating. Being a violinist at her church, she especially needed the ability to move her arms, head and neck. But every move was painful to the point where she contemplated giving up on ever playing again. She entered the Cnod™ 30-day trial and got almost an immediate emotional lift. After two weeks in the trial, the pain in her arm was gone and the pain in her neck and back were 85% improved. Her knees were the hotbed of the pain she experienced, but after 4 weeks wearing the Cnod™ the pain in her knees improved 70% to 75%. She said it was a comfort for her to know that there was someone praying when she was too emotionally distraught, or weary to pray for herself.

Martha & Marcia—CA

Marcia and Martha were our only mother/daughter trial participants. Martha said that her overall impression was that the Cnod™ worked for her. She had pain in her arm for more than a year. At times she could barely move it. After wearing the Cnod™ for 30 days, she reported that the pain in her arm was greatly reduced from being a sharp constant pain to a very dull periodic ache. She also commented that the Cnod™ helped her mother Marcia, who had been in an auto accident 15 years ago. Her mother, Marcia, injured her leg in the accident and was told by her physician that she would be in pain the rest of her life. For the past 15 years, every day her leg had been hurting. But after wearing the Cnod™ for 30 days, the pain in her leg was gone, and it has been sustained. She said her mother's attitude had completely changed. She became more positive and was pleased that the pain in her leg had left. I spoke with Martha a few days ago (nearly 5 months after her participation in the trial) and at age 96 her mother is still pain free. She wakes up in the morning asking for her Cnod™.

Along with this Martha stated that since wearing the Cnod™ she feels more relaxed and less stressful. She has started exercising. And whereas at one point she was depressed and dreaded getting out of bed, now she says she can face the day. She says the Cnod™ is still working for her.

Deborah—IN

A soldier in the army, Deborah was stationed in Iraq. There she endured many inconveniences and discomforts. Upon returning home after honorably serving her country, she had several carry-over affects from her time in Iraq and was subsequently diagnosed with post-traumatic stress disorder (PTSD). Many of her symptoms were inexplicable, but very real. When she would wake up in the morning her eyes would be bloodshot, so much so that she couldn't see clearly. Also, her right hand would swell shut during the night and it would take her an hour or more in the morning to work with her hand and loosen it up to where she could use it. After 3 days of wearing the Cnod™ she woke up early one morning to go to the bathroom with no problem. It wasn't until she was on her way back to her bed that she realized she could see. Her eyes were no longer bloodshot. Her vision, no longer blurred. The next day she also noticed that the swelling in her hand was gone. She had the full range of motion in her hand when she got out of bed that morning. And the progress has been sustained. She called me one morning during the 30-day trial and told me how happy she was and how peaceful she felt. She is still wearing the Cnod™ for other symptoms that remain.

Ryan—LA

Ryan is a world-class athlete and an Olympic hopeful. He fell just short of making the 2008 Olympic team in the high hurdles. Holder of numerous track records at one of the premier track universities in the U.S., he travels the world participating in numerous track and field contests. Two years ago he sustained a leg injury that could have jeopardized his career. He experienced pain in his left leg, in the right tendon attachment of the lower left hamstring. Edema had built up making the area at the hamstring stiff and hard. Although the injury was extremely painful he continued with the season. He had been to two different physical therapists for treatment. According to him neither of them was able to help his condition. He got a Cnod™ from his mother and took it to Trinidad with him for a race, wearing it at times when he was not running. He called and told me after two weeks with the Cnod™ that he ran his first race without pain in over two years, and also ran his best time ever. The type of injury he had takes a long time to heal. But his recovery was in his words "miraculous". One of his friends, another Olympic hopeful inquired about the Cnod™ and one was sent to him in Europe.

Byron—LA

For over 2½ years Byron had been staying at home in his bedroom watching TV all day. He seldom left his room for anything. His physician had diagnosed him with schizophrenia and placed him on medication. At 30 years of age, he lived with his mother, weighed over 300 lbs., and refused to honor any of his mother requests. Within the 2½ years, he attempted to work, but was unsuccessful in maintaining a job because of his illness. After hearing about the Cnod™, his mother asked if he could be a part of the study. Even though he did not fit our target, we agreed to give her one for him to wear. He started wearing the Cnod™ and after a week, to his mother's amazement he went out and mowed the lawn at her request. Then he began wearing the Cnod™ on his own, without his mother's coaxing.

He started reading the Bible on his own. After 3 weeks he began looking for jobs on his own. After 4 weeks Byron was once again allowed to drive a car after one year of not being allowed to. One day while he was out job hunting, he met one of his friends who invited him to church. He agreed to go to church with a friend, something he had not done in years. At the service he was born again, and was filled with the Spirit. After that he was willing to go to church with his mother. He attended church off and on with his mother before, but within the last six months had refused to attend church.

Now he studies the Bible with his mother—something he had never done. He is now interviewing for 3 jobs and at the time of this writing is in the final stages of the interview process for a management position at Walmart. After 2½ years of sitting alone in his room he has made this progress in less than 6 months. He still wears the Cnod™ and his mother says she has her son back. There is a light in his eyes again. His mother believes the use of the Cnod™ has brought about this sudden change in Byron's life along with the prayers of friends and family members. She says there were no other known variables brought into his life during this time that could possibly account for his sudden change except the Cnod™.

Appendix B

SCIENTIFIC STUDIES ON SPIRITUALITY AND HEALING PRAYER

• FEWER NEW AIDS-DEFINING ILLNESSES

A double-blind randomized trial of distant healing (remote prayer) in 40 patients with advanced AIDS found that after 6 months of prayer the treatment subjects acquired significantly fewer new AIDS-defining illnesses, had lower illness severity and required significantly fewer doctor visits, fewer hospitalizations and fewer days of hospitalization. Treated subjects also showed significantly improved mood compared with controls.

Sicher, F., Targ, E., Moore, D., Smith, H. S., "A Randomized Double-Blind Study of the Effect of Distant Healing in a Population with Advanced AIDS." Western Journal of Medicine 1998; Dec. 169 (6): 356-363

• LESS NEGATIVE EVENTS IN A CCU

A double-blind study of 393 patients at San Francisco General Medical Center found that coronary care unit (CCU) patients who received off site intercessory prayer subsequently had a significantly lower severity score based on the hospital course after entering. They required less ventilator assistance, fewer antibiotics and diuretics than the control patients.

Byrd, R. C., et al., "Positive Therapeutic Effects of Intercessory Prayer in a Coronary Care Unit Population," Southern Medical Journal 1988; Jul; 81 (7): 826-9.

• SURVIVING HEART SURGERY

A study of 232 patients at Dartmouth Medical School found that elderly heart patients were 14 times less likely to die following surgery if they found strength and comfort in their religious faith and remained socially involved.

Oxman, T. E. Freeman, D. H. Manheimer, E.D., "Lack of Social Participation or Religious Strength and Comfort as Risk Factors for Death after Cardiac Surgery in the Elderly." Psychosomatic Medicine 1995, 57(1), 5-15.

• PREVENTING HIGH BLOOD PRESSURE

Risk of diastolic hypertension ranked 40 percent lower among people who both attended religious services at least once a week and prayed or studied the Bible at least daily, Duke University researchers found in a study of nearly 4,000 people aged 65 years and older. These findings remained even after taking into account age, gender, race, education and other clinical factors that could affect blood pressure outcomes.

Koenig, H. G., et al., "The Relationship Between Religious Activities and Blood Pressure in Older Adults," International Journal of Psychiatry in Medicine 1998; 28(2): 189-213.

• IMPROVING IMMUNE FUNCTIONING

A pioneering study of more than 1,700 older adults from North Carolina conducted by researchers at Duke University Medical Center found that persons who attended church at least once a week were only half as likely as non-attendees to have elevated levels of interleukin-6, an immune system protein involved in a wide variety of age related diseases.

Koenig, H. G., et al., "Attendance at Religious Services, Interleukin-6, and Other Biological Parameters of Immune Function in Older Adults." International Journal of Psychiatry in Medicine 1997, 27(3): 233-250.

• RECOVERING FROM DEPRESSION

In a study of 87 depressed older adults hospitalized with medical illness, researchers at Duke University found the extent to which a patient's religious faith was a central motivating force in their lives, the faster they recovered from depression.

Koenig, H. G., George, L. K., Peterson, B. L., "Religiosity and Remission of Depression in Medically Ill Older Patients." American Journal of Psychiatry 1996, 155(4); 536-542.

• REDUCING LENGTH OF HOSPITAL STAYS

In a study of 542 patients aged 60 or older admitted consecutively to Duke University Medical Center, those who attended religious services weekly or more sliced hospital stays by more than half. People with no religious affiliation spent an average of 25 days in the hospital compared to 11 days for patients affiliated with some religious denomination. Patients who attended religious services weekly or more also were 43 percent less likely to have been hospitalized in the previous year.

Koenig, H. G., Larson, D. B., "Use of Hospital Services, Religious Attendance, and Religious Affiliation." Southern Medical Journal 1998; 91(10); 925-932.

• REDUCING RISK OF EARLIER DEATH

In a study that followed persons from a community for over 28 years, those who attended religious services weekly or more were 25 percent less likely to die than infrequent attendees. Not only were frequent attendees likely to live longer, once they began to attend church they also made healthier lifestyle choices, becoming more apt to quit smoking, to increase exercising, to expand their social support network and to stay married, noted the authors of this study of 5,286 people in Alameda County, California. Thus these health-enhancing behaviors of the religiously motivated seemed to contribute, at least in part, to their lower death rates.

Strawbridge, W. J., et. al., "Frequent Attendance at Religious Services and Mortality over 28 Years." American Journal of Public Health 1997; 87(6): 957-961.

• PREDICTING LONGER LIVES

Attending worship services on a regular basis was an important factor in predicting longevity in a study of 2,025 senior citizens living in Mann County, California. A range of other factors that might have contributed to health and living longer were taken into account, but attending religious services was found to be the most important predictive account.

Oman, D., Reed, D., "Religion and Mortality Among the Community-Dwelling Elderly." American Journal of Public Health 1998; 88(10): 1469-1476.

Appendix C

SPIRITUAL HEALING BIBLIOGRAPHY

Bonnke, Reinhard, **Mighty Manifestations,** Creation House, Orlando, Florida, 1994

Bosworth, F. F., **Christ the Healer,** Fleming H Revel Co., Westwood, NJ, 1983

Bridge, Donald, **Signs and Wonders Today,** Inter-Varsity Press, Leicester, England, 1985

Bubeck, Mark I. **The Adversary: The Christian Versus Demon Activity,** Moody, Chicago, IL, 1975

Cassidy, Michael, **Bursting the Wineskins,** Harold Shaw, Wheaton, IL 1983

Copeland, Gloria, **God's Prescription for Divine Health,** Kenneth Copeland Publications, Fort Worth, Texas, 1995

Deere, Jack, **Surprised by the Power of the Spirit,** Zondervan Publishing House, Grand Rapids, Michigan, 1993

Dossey, M.D., Larry, **Healing Words,** Harper, San Francisco, CA 1993

Dossey, M.D., Larry, **Prayer is Good Medicine,** Harper, San Francisco, CA 1996

Hagin, Kenneth E., **Zoe: The God-Kind of Life,** Faith Library Publications, Tulsa, Oklahoma, 1981

Hagin, Kenneth E., **What Faith Is,** Faith Library Publications, Tulsa, Oklahoma, 1980

Harper, Michael, **Spiritual Warfare, Recognizing and Overcoming the Work of Evil Spirits,** Servant Books, Ann Arbor, Michigan, 1970

Hinn, Benny, **The Anointing,** Thomas Nelson Publishers, Nashville, Tennessee, 1992

Horrorbin, Peter, **Healing Through Deliverance,** Sovereign World, England, 1991

Kelsey, Morton, T., **Healing and Christianity,** Harper and Rowe, San Francisco, CA 1973

Kenyon, E. W., **Jesus the Healer,** Kenyon Gospel Publishers, 1981

Lawrence, Roy, **Christian Healing Rediscovered: A Guide to Spiritual, Mental, Physical Wholeness,** Inter-Varsity Press, Downers Grove, IL, 1980

MacNutt, Francis, **Healing,** Ave Maria Press, Notre Dame, 1974

Mallone, George, **Those Controversial Gifts,** Inter-Varsity Press, Downers Grove, IL, 1983

Mc Crossan, T. J. **Bodily Healing and the Atonement,** Faith Library Publications, Tulsa, Oklahoma, 1986

McMillen, M.D., S. I., **None of these Diseases,** Fleming H. Revell Company, Westwood, New Jersey, 1963

Murray, Andrew, **With Christ in the School of Prayer,** Whitaker House, Springdale, Pennsylvania, 1981

Ogilvie, Lloyd John, **Why Not? Accept Christ's Healing and Wholeness,** Fleming Revell, Old Tappan, NJ, 1985

Osborne, T. L., **Healing the Sick: A Living Classic,** Harrison House, Tulsa, Oklahoma, 1986

Sanford, Agnes, **The Healing Light,** Macalester Park Publishing Co., St. Paul, MN, 1947

Smith, John W. V., **The Quest for Holiness and Unity: A Centennial History of the Church of God,** Warner Press, Anderson, Indiana, 1980

Stevens, Michael S., **Healing and Holiness in the Church of God Reformation Movement**, Scarecrow Press, Lanham, Maryland, 2008

Strong, James, S.T.D., LL.D., **Strong's Exhaustive Concordance,** Abingdon Press, Nashville, Tennessee, 1894 and 1986

Wagner, C. Peter, **Signs & Wonders Today,** Creation House, Altamonte Springs, Florida, 1987

Wagner, C. Peter, **Spirtual Power and Church Growth,** Strang Communications Company, Altamonte Springs, Florida, 1986

Wimber, John, **Power Evangelism,** Harper & Rowe, San Francisco, CA, 1986

Wimber, John, **Power Healing,** Harper & Rowe, San Francisco, CA, 1987

Whyte Maxwell, H. A., **The Power of the Blood,** Whitaker House, New Kensington, Pennsylvania, 1973

Appendix D

FAITH AND HEALING SCRIPTURE PASSAGES

Faith
Hebrews 11:1
Mt. 8:5–13
Mt. 15:21–28
Rom. 10:17
Mark 11:22–24

Gifts of the Spirit
1 Cor. 12:4–11
1 John 4:1
Mark 7:33
Mark 8:23

Healing Them All
Mt. 8:16–17
Mt. 12:15
Mt. 9:35
Psalm 103:3

Laying on of Hands
Mt. 8:3
Mt. 8:15
Mark 5:23
Mark 6:5
Mark 7:32
Mark 8:23-25
Luke 5:13
Hebrews 6:2
Mark 16:15-18
2 Tim. 1:6

Name and Person of Jesus
Ephesians 1:21-23
Philippians 2:9-11
Luke 10:18-22
Acts 3:1-8, 16
John 14:12-14

Our Position
2 Cor. 5:21
Ephesians 2:1

Power in Agreement
Mt. 18:19-20

Power in the Spirit
John 14:12-14
Acts 19:11

Power in Words

John 1:1–14
Psalm 119:130
Psalm 107:20
Acts 9:36–41

Power in Prayer
James 5:14–15
Acts 4:29–30
John 16:23–24
Mark 11:22–24
Mt. 18:19–20
Acts 9:36–41

Prayer and Anointing with Oil
James 5:14–15
Mark 6:13

Prophetic Scripture
Psalm 103:3
Isaiah 53:4–5
1 Peter 2:24
Isaiah 6:9–10
Mt. 13:14–15
Hebrews 9:27

Special Healing Power
Acts 19:11
Acts 5:14–16

Will of God in Healing
Mt. 8:16–17

Mt. 12:15
Mt. 9:35
Mal. 3:6
3 John 2
James 1:5-6
John 11:25
John 6:10
Exodus 15:26
Exodus 23:25
Deuteronomy 7:15
1 Cor. 15:16
Psalm 91:14-16

Send healing stories to:
eefoggs@live.com